M000314398

Way Down That Lonesome Road

Lonnie Johnson in Toronto, 1965-1970

BOOKS BY MARK MILLER

Jazz in Canada: Fourteen Lives (1982)

Boogie, Pete & The Senator: Canadian Musicians in Jazz, the Eighties (1987)

Cool Blues: Charlie Parker in Canada, 1953 (1989)

Such Melodious Racket: The Lost History of Jazz in Canada, 1914-1949 (1998)

The Miller Companion to Jazz in Canada (2001)

Some Hustling This! — Taking Jazz to the World, 1914-1929 (2005)

A Certain Respect for Tradition: Mark Miller on Jazz, Selected Writings 1980-2005 (2006)

High Hat, Trumpet and Rhythm: The Life and Music of Valaida Snow (2007)

Herbie Nichols: A Jazzist's Life (2009)

Way Down That Lonesome Road: Lonnie Johnson in Toronto, 1965-1970 (2011)

Way Down That Lonesome Road

Lonnie Johnson in Toronto, 1965-1970

Mark Miller

The Mercury Press & Teksteditions

Copyright © 2011 by Mark Miller

ALL RIGHTS RESERVED. No part of this book may be reproduced
by any means without the prior written permission of the publisher, with the exception of brief passages in reviews. Any request for photocopying or other reprographic copying of any part of this book must be directed in writing to ACCESS Copyright.

The publisher gratefully acknowledges the financial assistance of the Canada Council for the Arts, the Ontario Arts Council, the Ontario Media Development Corporation, and the Ontario Book Publishing Tax Credit Program. The publisher further acknowledges the financial support of the Government of Canada through the Department of Canadian Heritage's Book Publishing Industry Development Program (BPIDP) for our publishing activities.

Canadä

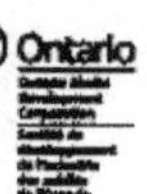

Thanks also to the OAC's Arts Investment Fund.

Editor: Beverley Daurio
Composition and page design: Beverley Daurio
Cover design: Mark Miller and Beverley Daurio
Cover photograph: Lonnie Johnson at the Golden Nugget, Toronto, in 1968. Photograph by Bill Smith. Courtesy Bill Smith.

Title page photograph: Lonnie Johnson, publicity shot, 1960s. Courtesy Roberta Barrett.

Library and Archives Canada Cataloguing in Publication
Miller, Mark, 1951-
Way down that lonesome road : Lonnie Johnson in Toronto 1965-1970 / Mark Miller.
Includes index.
Also issued in electronic format.
ISBN 978-0-9868696-4-8
1. Johnson, Lonnie, 1899-1970. 2. Jazz musicians--United States--Biography. 3. Guitarists--United States--Biography. 4. Jazz musicians--Canada--Biography. 5. Guitarists--Canada--Biography. I. Title.
ML419.J628M54 2011 787.87'165092 C2011-901673-7

Mercury print edition: ISBN 978-1-55128-148-3

The Mercury Press / Teksteditions
Box 672, Station P, Toronto, Ontario Canada M5S 2Y4
www.themercurypress.ca & www.teksteditions.com

In memory of John Norris
1934-2010

Table of Contents

i. Preface

I want all you people to listen to my song
I want all you people to listen to my song
Remember me after all the days I'm gone

— *Mr. Johnson's Blues,* 1925

So sang Lonnie Johnson on the very first recording that he made under his own name, 86 years ago in St. Louis, mindful even then of his own mortality. If he has indeed been remembered after all the days, and now decades, since his death, 41 years ago in Toronto, it has been largely for his early and essential contribution to the histories of both blues and jazz.

He was an original among singers and guitarists in the 1920s and, for that, he was influential in the years that followed. But originality and influence exist only in the abstract; they offer no sense of the man himself, no sense of the personal qualities suggested parenthetically on the invitation to a wake that was held in Toronto several months after his death.

"For Lonnie's real friends," the invitation read, "(those who knew all about him & loved him just the same)."[1]

He was a gentle soul, a charmer and a ladies' man. He could be too trusting, an easy mark, but he was also rather sly, feigning innocence and playing for sympathy when it served his purpose. He looked out for himself first and foremost, but he could be generous toward others. He was regarded with respect, great affection and, occasionally, exasperation.

These, at least, are among the memories of some of the many people whose paths he crossed in Toronto between 1965 and 1970, the final years of his life — the years that serve as the time frame for this book.

As much, however, as *Way Down That Lonesome Road* is a biographical study of Lonnie Johnson in this period, it is also a social and cultural history of the scene that he encountered in Toronto. As such, it takes its lead from my book *Cool Blues*,[2] which found in the visits of the legendary alto saxophonist Charlie Parker to Montreal and Toronto in 1953 an opportunity to bring the modern jazz communities in each of those cities back to life. And like *Cool Blues*, *Way Down That Lonesome Road* (which takes its title from a song that Johnson recorded in 1928) is populated by a cast of secondary characters — musicians, critics, friends and fans — who have stories of their own to tell.

Charlie Parker was in Canada for only a few nights altogether in 1953, but one of those nights found him at Massey Hall in a performance with Dizzy Gillespie, Bud Powell, Charles Mingus and Max Roach that would be immortalized as The Greatest Jazz Concert Ever. Johnson, who stayed in Toronto for almost five full years, also performed at Massey Hall, making a cameo appearance in a blues concert, headlined by Bobby "Blue" Bland and Buddy Guy, that would have been lost to history were it not for his presence on the bill — for the two songs that he sang, for the point in his life when he sang them and for the tumultuous response that they generated.

I was there on that February evening in 1970, an 18-year-old blues fan forever fortunate to have witnessed what was surely the crowning moment of Johnson's time in Toronto, and to have felt the surge of emotion that filled the hall first when he moved slowly to centre stage and again when he returned, even more slowly, to the wings. It was the only time that I heard him in person.

Johnson, of course, performed on many other nights in Toronto — nights at the Penny Farthing when he held his audience at rapt attention, and nights at Steele's Tavern when he was all but ignored. He took the good with the bad. He was a proud man, but he was also practical. And he could be philosophical.

When asked in 1967, at what would be his final recording session, whether anyone was working on a biography about him, he said no, and added mildly that in any event writers seemed to have their own ideas — or rather, their own *idea* — of how his story should be told. "They look for me mostly to tell the hardships of my life," he remarked, "instead of the best part of my life..."[3]

The story of his years in Toronto combines both — the happiest of times and the hardest, a Dickensian sort of paradox, albeit in a tale of just one city. This is that tale; here is that city.

Mark Miller
Toronto, July 2011

1. "An authentic living legend"

Lonnie Johnson would have had little reason to pause at the top of the half dozen steps down to the New Gate of Cleve, little reason save perhaps to double-check the street number of the Avenue Road coffeehouse, 45A, and — ever a man with an eye for the female form — to glance at the dresses on display in the window of couturier Lena Lascelles' Maison Française upstairs at 45. Summer dresses, in fact — although summer itself was still a month away on this mild evening, the third Thursday of May 1965.

No, Johnson would have had little reason to expect that the next four nights at the New Gate of Cleve might be much different than many of the other engagements that he had taken in a career of more than 50 years — little reason to think that *this* engagement might in fact be a turning point in his life.

True, he could not have anticipated how *few* people would come to hear him. The New Gate of Cleve was in only its third week at its new Avenue Road address and its young owners seemed not to appreciate the significance of their latest attraction. They had advertised "The Rhythm and Blues Sounds of Lonnie Johnson" in the Toronto *Telegram* that day,[1] a description that referred to what was perhaps the least of Johnson's many accomplishments as a singer and guitarist in the recorded history of blues and jazz — a description, moreover, that made him appear to be an even greater anomaly than he really was among the folk and blues acts that usually performed at the club.

But Johnson had faced small audiences before. Indeed, there had been times when he faced no audiences at all — times when he was forced to work outside of music, taking care not to harm his hands even as he subjected them of necessity to the perils of manual labour.

Those times were over. Johnson had been making his living again as a musician ever since a radio announcer in Philadelphia, Chris Albertson, found him in 1960 employed locally as a janitor. Johnson quickly resumed his recording career and began appearing in nightspots as different as the Playboy Club in Chicago and Gerde's Folk City in New York's Greenwich Village. A tour in Europe with other blues greats followed late in 1963.

Johnson also visited Canada that year, working in Hamilton at the Downstairs on King Street West for four nights over the Easter weekend.[2] He had likely crossed the border at least once before, appearing in the early 1920s with the vaudevillians Glenn & Jenkins at the Orpheum theatres in Winnipeg and Vancouver. But Canadian cities were not routinely on the circuit travelled by veteran bluesmen until the 1960s, when the survivors among them — most, like Johnson, newly rediscovered — were drawn into the revival of American folk music more generally and took their place at festivals and in clubs alongside veteran white traditionalists and younger white singers and songwriters.

So it was that Johnson had shared a bill at Gerde's Folk City in March 1965 with the young Canadian singer Bonnie Dobson, whose song *Morning Dew* was just then catching the fancy of her contemporaries. And so it was that Johnson followed Toronto's Gordon Lightfoot and a New York couple, Richard and Mimi Farina, into the New Gate of Cleve. Lightfoot's first single, *I'm Not Saying*, had just been released; Lightfoot and the Farinas were only weeks away from their debut appearances at the important Newport Folk Festival in Rhode Island.

THE *OLD* GATE OF CLEVE, as it were, had operated for a year or so at 161 Dupont Street, several blocks to the north of the new location, a few blocks more to the west, and altogether too many blocks from the Yorkville "scene" that had lately centralized around the intersection of Yorkville Avenue proper and Avenue Road.

Yorkville in 1965, and for a few years before and after, served Toronto much as Greenwich Village served New York and Haight-Ashbury served San Francisco, a neighbourhood where members of the "hippie" counterculture of the day lived, worked and played — musicians, painters, writers, draft resisters, runaway teens and social activists, all in their way trying to change the world. Or, if not *the* world, at least *their* world.

Yorkville was comparatively small by New York and San Francisco standards, residential in design and Victorian in detail, reflecting its origins as a mid-19th-century village on what at the time were the northern outskirts of Toronto. Several of its coffeehouses offered music within a stroll of no more than a minute or two from the New Gate of Cleve, including the Riverboat, El Patio, Penny Farthing and Mousehole east along Yorkville, and the Half Beat, Purple Onion, Devil's Den and Village Corner up and down Avenue Road. That is, a stroll of no more than a minute or two when the sidewalks were clear of the teenagers who flocked to the Village, as it was known, from other parts of the city every night — "hundreds of kids," as Sheila Gormley described them in the Toronto *Telegram* that summer, "jammed together and moving down the street like a cockeyed centipede."[3]

Came Saturday night, cars on Yorkville Avenue could take 20 minutes to inch along the two relatively short blocks from Bay Street west to Avenue Road, there to turn south for Bloor Street, then east back to Bay, there to begin the crawl again.

The crush of people on the sidewalks did not spill over, however, into the New Gate of Cleve, whose slow start in its first few weeks at its new address was a portent of its struggle to stay open in face of Yorkville's move away from folk, blues and jazz to rock, a struggle that the room lost in less than a year. After it reopened in May 1966 as Boris's, it was home to a succession of the city's better rock bands, notably the Ugly Ducklings, Luke and the Apostles and Kensington Market.

For the moment, though, Richard and Mimi Farina sang at the Gate to an audience of six during a set reviewed by Sid Adilman for the New York show business tabloid *Variety*.[4] Lonnie Johnson had two listeners *fewer* when Patrick Scott, the jazz critic for *The Globe and Mail*, stopped by the following week. "When I departed an hour later his audience had doubled," Scott reported with evident satisfaction, "and I had heard a performance so profoundly moving that its memory will haunt me forever."[5]

Scott returned two nights later with his entire family as well as a couple of friends and two visiting American pianists who were enjoying nights off from their respective engagements at the Golden Nugget and the Chez Paree, Don Ewell and Sir Charles Thompson — all "as insurance that Sunday night's audience would be at least as large as Friday's."

Scott was a crusty, old-school journalist of the H.L. Mencken persuasion, reviled by local and visiting musicians alike for the blunt, often dismissive and occasionally vicious tone of his reviews. But he also had his favourites, as Johnson — "an authentic living legend" — was from the very first.

"I am about to use the word I try to employ more sparingly than any other in my vocabulary," Scott announced in his report from the New Gate of Cleve, alluding to his customary severity as a critic by way of prefacing his assertion that Johnson was nothing less than "an artist." To which he added proudly, "And I regard it as an honor to have heard him."

The honour was ultimately shared by just a few others at the Gate, although their number included a future rock star then still in his teens, the guitarist and singer Neil Young,[6] and a British jazz aficianado in his early thirties, John Norris, who managed the jazz, blues and folk department at Sam the Record Man on Yonge Street and edited *Coda Magazine*, then in its seventh year. Norris would devote his life quietly and conscientiously to jazz, putting the integrity of the music on its own terms before all other considerations.

While Young's reaction to Johnson's performance has gone unrecorded, Norris suggested in *Coda Magazine* that — Patrick Scott to the contrary — those in attendance at the Gate "who remember[ed Johnson] for the fine blues he used to sing were in for a shock as his whole act was geared to that of a cabaret show." Norris described Johnson's voice as "strong" and his guitar work as "really good," but noted that "when he did sing a blues it was without any kind of conviction or feeling" and added that a certain sameness pervaded the entire performance.[7]

By the time Norris' dissenting opinion appeared in the June/July issue of *Coda Magazine*, however, Johnson had returned for a month at the Penny Farthing, an engagement that was as triumphant as his four nights at the New Gate of Cleve had been disappointing.

No matter that he had a young daughter back in Philadelphia, he rarely left Toronto again.

2. "Nice plain people"

The New Gate of Cleve was just a stone's throw north across Avenue Road from the Park Plaza Hotel, whose rooftop Plaza Room had been the musical home during the early 1950s to the first African-American musician of note to settle in Toronto for any length of time, pianist Calvin Jackson.

Unlike Lonnie Johnson, Jackson was a musical sophisticate, educated in the late 1930s at the Juilliard School of Music in New York and employed in the late 1940s by Metro-Goldwyn-Mayer in Hollywood. During his years in Toronto, 1950 to 1956, he enjoyed the highest profile of any of the city's jazz musicians, black or white, starring in 1953 on his own weekly CBC-TV series, *Jazz with Jackson*, and appearing as a soloist and conductor with the Toronto Symphony Orchestra.

Jackson was drawn to Toronto by what he perceived to be the relative absence of racism in the city — relative at least to the degree of discrimination that he had experienced as an African-American in the United States. The local media did not hesitate to record his impressions on this count, flattering as they were to Toronto; the praise of an American would always be well-received in Canada, particularly if it came in comparison to anything American — and all the more to anything as central to the American experience as racism.

Jackson spoke of "the sanctity of personality"[1] that he had felt in Toronto when he worked at the Casino early in 1950. That engagement complete, he flew home to New York, retrieved his dog, his car and his personal effects and drove back to Canada within days.

"For the second time in my life," he explained later, perhaps implying that the first time had been his engagement at the Casino, "I was not conscious of being different from other people. I walked along the streets and felt as though I belonged with those who passed by; I entered restaurants and found that the people there didn't raise their eyebrows; I asked directions and was given a polite and uncondescending answer."[2]

If anything, Jackson's race offered him a professional advantage in Toronto, where resident black performers of his renown were rare enough in the 1950s to be regarded — and no doubt patronized, in both senses of the word — as exotic. Among Jackson's African-*Canadian* contemporaries at the time, performers also in their thirties, only the singer Phyllis Marshall enjoyed similar prominence on the CBC and in local nightclubs, while Cy McLean played piano more obscurely in the city's taverns and strip joints. A younger generation of musicians, including the pianists Wray Downes and Connie Maynard and the drummer Archie Alleyne, was just beginning to emerge in the early 1950s from the small black community that shared the working-class neighbourhood around Spadina Avenue and College Street with Jewish and Italian families.

Soon enough, though, Jackson exhausted the opportunities that Toronto offered a musician of his skill and range. "They weren't making records there or films, you know," he noted in 1959, looking back from Hollywood on his decision to return to the United States. "There was no room for expansion."[3]

THE WARMTH of Calvin Jackson's welcome as a black musician in Toronto was neither the exception nor the rule. When several young African-Americans with hard-bop inclinations joined some of their local counterparts in the operation of the after-hours MINC (Musicians Incorporated) Club above a bakery on Parliament Street briefly in 1959 and again above a dress shop on Yonge Street even more briefly in early 1960, they found themselves subject to police raids, arrests and finally, in August 1960, deportation. Jackson, of course, had been the model of respectability; the MINC Club was conversely presumed by local authorities to be a haven for drug use and prostitution, an assumption perhaps based on nothing more than its principals' race.[4]

By the time Lonnie Johnson arrived in 1965, nine years after Jackson's departure, the visibility of black performers in Toronto had increased only slightly, although the patterns of Caribbean immigration that would change the face of the city in the years to follow were already in evidence.

Canada's most celebrated jazz musician, Oscar Peterson, had moved to Toronto from Montreal in 1958, but for the most part worked internationally, limiting his local appearances to concerts and to the occasional engagement at the Town Tavern on Queen Street East, which otherwise served with the nearby Colonial Tavern on Yonge Street as a stop, a week or two at a time, on the circuit travelled by American musicians.

One of those musicians, the pianist Sir Charles Thompson, had taken a year-long engagement at the Chez Paree on Bloor Street west of Avenue Road, while the singers Salome Bey, Jodie Drake, Ada Lee and Almeta Speaks, all Toronto residents by 1965, found receptive audiences for their jazz and blues stylings in various other nightspots. A sixth African-American entertainer, the singer Olive Brown, was a favourite at the Golden Nugget on Yonge Street just below Bloor, and a seventh, Frank

Jimmy Rushing (left), Lonnie Johnson, Olive Brown, Toronto, May 1966. Photograph by James Lewcun. Courtesy *The Globe and Mail.*

Motley, noted for playing two trumpets at once, worked with his Motley Crew in the rhythm-and-blues clubs that flourished even farther south on Yonge Street.

One of Motley's singers, the transvestite Jackie Shane, had considerable radio exposure locally in 1963 with his recording of *Any Other Way*, as did the Canadian singer Shirley Matthews with her version of *Big Town Boy*. Still other black American and Canadian singers — Dianne Brooks, Jackie Gabriel, Jack Hardin, Shawne and Jay Jackson, Eric Mercury — were heard along Yonge Street with Toronto's own rhythm-and-blues bands. Meanwhile, the Canadian folksingers Al Cromwell and Jackie Washington enjoyed modest profiles in Yorkville coffeehouses, home also to a teenaged Rick James, who spent 1965 and early 1966 singing as Ricky Matthews with the Mynah Birds while AWOL from the US Navy.

Among Toronto's jazz musicians, Wray Downes was back from a sojourn in Europe, where he had played with the expatriate American stars Sidney Bechet, Buck Clayton and Bill Coleman; Archie Alleyne boasted a similarly impressive list of credits as the house drummer intermittently since 1955 at the Town Tavern. Other young, African-Canadian jazz musicians, however, were limited largely by opportunity to playing rhythm and blues, although one of their number, guitarist Sonny Greenwich, soon left them behind, and eclipsed the city's white modernists as well, when he embraced the avant-garde influence, stylistically and spiritually, of John Coltrane.

Inevitably, all of these musicians encountered racism in some form or other in Toronto; discrimination, however subtle in comparison to its virulence in many parts of the United States, was by no means absent, even if Lonnie Johnson, no less than Calvin Jackson and the other Americans who had been hardened by lifelong experience at home, might have thought its sting comparatively mild, perhaps even to the point where they felt it not at all. Johnson, for one, took at face value the response of the landlords he approached when at one point he was in need of lodging. "It's funny," he told a friend who knew better, "they all want women for roomers — not men."[5]

If Jackson had benefitted professionally from his apparent respectability on his arrival in Toronto, Johnson had a similar advantage by virtue of his venerability. Landlords aside, his welcome in the city was very warm indeed.

"I've found me a new home," he told an American interviewer one year later, echoing Jackson's sentiments, if not quite his eloquence. "I love Canada. Everybody here is nice plain people. I have found more happiness the last few months in Canada than I have all my life."[6]

3. "Tough to follow"

Toronto was Lonnie Johnson's last stop in a career of stops, at least the eighth city in which he had lived for any length of time. "I'm a roamin' rambler," he sang rather presciently in his *Roaming Rambler Blues* during the mid-1920s, embracing an image that was popular among blues singers of the day. "I ramble and roam everywhere."[1]

He set out at some point in the late 1910s from New Orleans, where he was born Alonzo Johnson on the 8th of February 1889, 1894, 1899 or 1900. This last, recorded on his application for US Social Security, was his year of preference by the time he had reached Toronto, its double zeroes simplifying the calculation of his age and, once that calculation had been made, leaving him still young enough to be prized by the ladies — always a consideration in Johnson's mind. "I got a gal in Texas," he boasted in the third stanza of *Roaming Rambler Blues*. "I got gals in Tennessee." Soon enough, he had gals in Toronto, too.

His age was just one of many variables in the stories that he told of his life. While he could be reasonably forthcoming when questioned by interviewers about his career, he was not especially consistent, instead displaying a free and fanciful attitude toward the dates and order of significant events and offering wild exaggerations as to their duration.

In a 1967 interview with Moses Asch of Folkways Records, for example, he squeezed more than 25 years of work both in and out of music between his first blues recordings for OKeh in — *his* date — 1920 and his first jazz recordings with Louis Armstrong in — as history documents it — 1927. Five years with OKeh, five in an East St. Louis steel mill, five as a violinist with Charlie Creath on Mississippi River steamers, three in a Peoria, Illinois, nightclub and seven in a Peoria foundry — as well as stints manhandling railway ties in a creosote plant and maintaining the greens at a golf course. That done, Johnson told Asch, he then spent 11 years on the B.F. Keith vaudeville circuit.[2]

Thus Johnson in 1967. A few years earlier, though, in an interview with the British blues historian Paul Oliver, he estimated his OKeh contract at 11 years, his time with Charlie Creath at seven and his association with the vaudevillians Glenn & Jenkins, a Keith act, at four.[3]

Some of Johnson's assertions can be substantiated, some disproved. Others remain beyond verification. Nothing has been found, for example, to document the time that he claimed to have spent with a revue in England during the First World War, or to support his lament that, in his absence abroad, his entire family, save for his brother James, died of the flu — ostensibly in the pandemic that swept North America in 1918.

All of these things may well have happened. Indeed many of them most certainly did, though perhaps not quite as dramatically or for as long as Johnson suggested — ever, it seems, trying to impress. How else to explain his boasts during the 1960s that, previous assertions notwithstanding, his mother was in fact still very much alive and in her nineties?[4]

Some of his assertions seem safe enough, their accuracy in any case of no great importance one way or the other. His family, he said, was large and musical, sufficiently so on both counts that his father, whom he once described as a shoemaker,[5] was able to assemble a string band that performed for weddings, dances and other social functions. The band's existence is corroborated by bassist George "Pops" Foster, who heard Johnson playing guitar on street corners "all over New Orleans" with one of his brothers and their father, both violinists.[6]

Another Crescent City jazz musician, trumpeter Ernest "Punch" Miller, spoke of working with Johnson in the small town of Raceland and along the nearby Bayou Lafourche, southwest of New Orleans, which would likely have been as close as the young guitarist came to the sort of rural experience that shaped the lives and music of so many of his contemporaries among the "country" blues singers whose popularity during the 1920s parallelled his. Miller and Johnson ran together for about three years; Miller later dated the time frame implicitly, if incompletely, when he identified one of the items in their repertoire of blues and popular melodies as *Beautiful Doll* — presumably *Oh, You Beautiful Doll*, a song not in circulation until 1911.[7]

Johnson's travels with Miller aside, he was a city boy. He was also — according to Pops Foster — "the only guy we had around New Orleans who could play jazz guitar." There were other guitarists in the city's early jazz bands, of course, including Foster's brother Willie, as well as Emile "Stalebread" Lacoume, Stonewall Matthews, Johnny St. Cyr, Bud Scott and two men who worked at one time or another around 1900 with the legendary cornetist Buddy Bolden — Brock Mumford and Lorenzo Staulz. But Foster made particular note of Johnson's ability to "take off on a number" — to improvise — and suggested rather ambiguously that he was "tough to follow."[8]

To wit, a tough *act* to follow or a tough musician to *accompany*? Either way, Johnson's skills clearly made an impression on his fellow musicians — his skills *and* his versatility. As was common practice among guitarists of the day in New Orleans, he also played banjo; in truth, most of his contemporaries were banjoists first, guitarists second. But Johnson's proficiency extended further to violin and piano; he played one or the other on several of his early blues recordings for OKeh in 1925 and 1926, alternating between the two instruments with his brother James, who was similarly accomplished.

Naturally, a musician capable of applying himself to a variety of instruments would likely also be adaptable to a variety of musical styles, in Johnson's case to *the* variety of musical styles that flourished in New Orleans, that most cosmopolitan of American cities — whether blues and rags, both on their own terms and as they were being embraced by jazz in its early years, or the Cuban influences and the "Spanish tinge" more generally that flowed north across the Gulf of Mexico, or again the principles of melody and harmony that were sustained by the Creole musicians of New Orleans in their veneration of all things European.

Not that Johnson necessarily mastered each of these styles in detail. But his awareness of them — if only in passing, if only because they were "in the air" as part of the city's rich musical culture — would have offered him a broader frame of musical reference in his formative years than that available to other blues singers and guitarists in theirs. Most of his rivals in the late 1920s tended to be rustics whose styles were identified with a state or a region — be it Texas, the Mississippi Delta or the Piedmont — and were shaped by the immediate and inherently parochial influence of other rustics who were simply working their way back and forth through the same area. While they did not limit themselves to blues, at least not until they began to record, they were no match for Johnson in terms of their range.

"We played anything [people] wanted to hear," he once explained, itemizing the repertoire on which he and his brother James drew as "ragtime melodies, sweet songs, waltzes — that kind of thing. A lot of people liked opera, so we did some of that, too."[9]

Clearly, Johnson was on a different path from the beginning than his contemporaries. That path might very well have taken him to England during the First World War; it most certainly took him by the early 1920s into vaudeville, where he appears to have started very near the top, albeit in a supporting role, when he travelled on the "big time" B.F. Keith circuit with the popular African-American song, dance and comedy team Glenn & Jenkins.

William Glenn and Walter Jenkins appeared in blackface as porters in "Working for the Railroad," a routine that found them, brooms in hand, sweeping out a mock train station. For good measure, Jenkins played "the 'bluest' harmonica... ever heard in vaudeville."[10]

Johnson was not billed by name in the act but may have been present in January 1922 when it was reviewed at the Palace Theater in New York for *Variety*. The reporter, one "Ibee.," who had apparently seen Glenn & Jenkins before, took note of the changes that they had made to the act, in particular the banjo solo that they had added.

"It was played by a third member," Ibee. wrote, "but that was not noticed until Glenn and Jenkins appeared from the opposite wings. The new 'boy' was out for the finish with his instrument, accompanying the team for a new version of the sweeping song and dance..."[11] A review of the act in Winnipeg later in 1922 made favourable reference to its "harmony on the mouth organ and guitar."[12]

Glenn & Jenkins were among the select few African-American acts booked by the Keith organization and its affiliates in the northern and western states, in Canada and along the Eastern seaboard — everywhere, in fact, save the south. Such employment was prized for its prestige and comparatively civil working conditions by African-American entertainers, who were otherwise limited — as Johnson soon enough found for himself — to smaller, hardscrabble circuits, notably the TOBA (Theater Owners' Booking Association) chain of mostly second- and third-rate theatres that catered to black audiences in the south, southwest and midwest, as well as in a few of the larger northern cities.

Johnson's memories of his TOBA experiences during the 1920s were mixed: "You do five, six shows a day; you got little money, but everybody's happy." He had started, he once said, at the Standard Theater in Philadelphia and "went as far as TOBA can carry you."[13] The African-American press offered the occasional report as to the whereabouts of one Alonzo Johnson, noting for example that he was working in Florida with Charles "Fats" Hayden during the fall of 1923 as a member of Riddick and Santanar's 100 Pound Girl Company,[14] and that he was appearing elsewhere in the south with Mary Hicks a year later as two of Leola Grant's Plaza Players. Both Hayden and Grant later recorded as blues singers; so too did Johnson's wife in the late 1920s, whose name — coincidentally or not — was Mary.[15]

Grant's Players were at the Vendome Theater in Hot Springs, Arkansas, when they came under the scrutiny of Hi Tom Long, a local correspondent for *Billboard* and the Chicago *Defender*. "Johnson and Hicks, Alonzo and Mary," Long wrote in the latter publication, "opened with *Going South,* also introducing some fast cross-fire comedy lines that were thoroughly clean [i.e., not salacious] in every respect. Mary Hicks [sang] *Some Day* [sic] *Sweetheart*, while Johnson did *The Jelly Roll Blues*; [they closed] with a nifty routine of buck, wing and clog dancing..."[16]

Alonzo Johnson continued to travel with Mary Hicks in Texas, Louisiana and Oklahoma during the winter of 1924-5. Off the road, meanwhile, he — assuming Alonzo and Lonnie were one and the same Johnson — gravitated toward St. Louis. When Lonnie Johnson entered a "blues singing contest" there at the Booker Washington Theater in February 1924, he was living in Lovejoy, Illinois, a small African-American community on the northern outskirts of East St. Louis, across the Mississippi River from St. Louis proper.[17]

Johnson later insisted that he had won the Booker Washington Theater contest — that he had taken first prize for 18 weeks straight, and that his success led to his recording contract with OKeh,[18] the first label of several in the early 1920s to introduce a "race" series of blues and gospel releases intended expressly for the African-American market. And indeed the contest did run for 18 weeks, beginning in November 1923, with an OKeh contract as its grand prize. Johnson, however, was not among the initial 31 entrants identified by the local African-American newspaper, the St. Louis *Argus*.[19]

Most of the hopefuls were in fact female, reflecting the predominance of women among early blues recording stars, from Mamie Smith with her groundbreaking *Crazy Blues* in 1920 through Ethel Waters, Trixie Smith and Edith Wilson in 1921 to Bessie Smith and Gertrude "Ma" Rainey in 1923, a matriarchy that remained unchallenged until Papa Charlie Jackson, Blind Lemon Jefferson and Johnson himself had *their* first hits — Jackson in 1925 and Jefferson and Johnson in 1926.

Johnson in any event qualified for the finals at the Booker Washington Theater only in mid-February 1924 and ultimately *lost* two weeks later to another St. Louis performer, Irene Scruggs, whom OKeh recorded — as promised — soon after in New York.[20]

Johnson would wait another 20 months to make his first recordings for OKeh, the invitation to do so likely coming from the company's St. Louis talent scout, Jesse J. Johnson, an entrepreneurial figure who owned the Deluxe Music Shoppe on Market Street and promoted social events in local halls, including the Paradise Dance Palace, and on Mississippi steamers, notably the *St. Paul.* Foremost among the musicians in Jesse Johnson's regular employ during the mid-1920s was the East St. Louis cornetist Charlie Creath; it was with Creath's Jazz-O-Maniacs, albeit reduced in number from eight to four, that Lonnie Johnson appeared as a singer and violinist on a single OKeh side, *Won't Don't Blues*, in the very first days of November 1925.

Creath's recordings have been largely overlooked in the early histories of both jazz and blues despite their rarity on not one count, but two. Creath and his musicians played in the New Orleans style that cornetist King Oliver had taken to Chicago and that had doubled back, likely via Oliver's recordings for Gennett and OKeh, to St. Louis. Uniquely, though, at a time when the public was particularly captivated by the sound of women singing the blues to the accompaniment of jazz musicians, Creath chose to feature the voices of men — in particular the Jazz-O-Maniacs' drummer, Floyd Campbell, rather gruff on the band's first two sessions, and Johnson, in a light, keening tenor on the third. Creath, moreover, gave similarly unexpected exposure on *Won't Don't Blues* to the violin, an instrument theretofore found on scant few recordings either of jazz or blues and fewer still in the slippery "hot" style that Johnson employed in alternation with himself as he sang each new line of the song's lyrics.

Johnson's next recordings, and his earliest for OKeh under his own name, *Mr. Johnson's Blues* and *Falling Rain Blues*, followed within days, the first again an oddity of sorts in the history of blues and jazz to the mid-1920s. Johnson sang just three lines in *Mr. Johnson's Blues* — "I want all you people to listen to my song/I want all you people to listen to my song/Remember me after all the days I'm gone" — and took the first, second, third and fifth of the remaining five choruses to show off his prowess as a guitarist. He gave the fourth chorus to his pianist at the session, John Arnold, who was a member of the Jazz-O-Maniacs' primary competition among St. Louis jazz bands in 1925, Bennie Washington's Six Aces.[21]

OKeh already listed six solo guitar rags by Sylvester Weaver of Louisville, Kentucky, in its catalogue, the earliest of them dating to late 1923. In *Mr. Johnson's Blues*, however, OKeh had a performance of rather greater sophistication in its blend of blues form and jazz improvisation, even if the label's publicity campaign missed, or misrepresented, the recording's selling points. "Linger and laugh and listen to Lonnie sing 'Mr. Johnson's Blues,'" read an ad for the recording in the Chicago *Defender*, putting its emphasis on that one unrevealing stanza of lyrics. "And say," it added, as if no more than an afterthought, "there's a blue accompaniment that keeps your feet keeping time."[22]

Johnson continued during his seven years as an OKeh recording artist to move easily, influentially and with neither precedent nor parallel between what historians would define retrospectively as "classic blues" and "classic jazz." He recorded more than 90 blues issued under his own name and many more in tandem with Clara Smith, Victoria Spivey, Clarence Williams and Spencer Williams; he also appeared on record as a guitarist or violinist with several other singers, including Texas Alexander and, betraying OKeh briefly in favour of Vocalion, Luella Miller. Johnson's jazz sides, meanwhile, were far fewer but even more significant in their way: duets with the white jazz guitarist Eddie Lang — OKeh billed Lang as Blind Willie Dunn in order to disguise his identity for the "race" market — and cameos with Louis Armstrong's Hot Five, the Duke Ellington Orchestra and Don Redman's Chocolate Dandies, the last better known as McKinney's Cotton Pickers.

Johnson brought style to the substance of the blues, a degree of finish that was almost antithetical to the rougher esthetic of his contemporaries. As such, he anticipated the sophistication of younger musicians, most notably B.B. King, who acknowledged both Johnson and the Texas singer and guitarist Blind Lemon Jefferson as early, important and admittedly dichotomous influences. Johnson, wrote King in his autobiography *Blues All around Me*, "took a left turn where Blind Lemon went right. Where Blind Lemon was raw, Lonnie was gentle. Lonnie was more sophisticated. His voice was lighter and sweeter, more romantic, I'd say. He had a dreamy quality to his singing and a lyrical way with the guitar."[23]

Not for Johnson the harshness of the rural blues singer. Though his voice was characteristically nasal and, as such, clear and penetrating, his light tremolo and relaxed delivery softened its clarion quality to plaintive effect. His songs, or rather his lyrics, explored the standard themes of the blues, from bedbugs to bad women, each in a personal and inventively poetic manner that ranged in attitude from the melancholic to the moralistic and on to the misogynistic, the last perhaps in response —

variously quizzical and embittered — to the eventual foundering of his first marriage. He was also no stranger to the sexual double entendres that were popular in the 1920s; his version with Victoria Spivey of *Toothache Blues*, which required two sides of a 78 RPM recording to exhaust all of its central metaphor's possibilities, was among his most successful.

In turn, Johnson's guitar work was trim and technically advanced both for the day and for the blues. He was infallibly deft and often quite dazzling, despite a repetitive streak and a notable allegiance to the key of "D." So obvious was his instrumental skill that OKeh — having misjudged *Mr. Johnson's Blues* — finally realized that his guitar style might be saleable in and of itself. Still, OKeh marketed his first solo piece, the boastful *To Do This You Gotta Know How* from 1926, only to white record buyers and then left several of his solo recordings from 1927 unissued altogether. In December 1927, however, it added Johnson in a strictly instrumental capacity to two sessions by Louis Armstrong's Hot Five.

Armstrong credited OKeh's "Mr. Fern" with the idea for what appears to have been an early instance of "cross-promotion" — the pairing of two artists on the same label in the hope of drawing them to the attention of each other's fans. Years later, Armstrong remembered having no objections to the scheme; he had first heard Johnson in New Orleans in 1915, he said, and admitted that he "always wanted to make a record with Lonnie."[24] In fact he made five — three in 1927 and two more in March 1929.

Johnson was prominent on four. For the most part he remained in character, a blues guitarist among jazz musicians. His contributions to *I'm Not Rough* and *Savoy Blues* would have been appropriate to any of his own recordings, although the urgent tremolo that he employed in the ensembles on *I'm Not Rough* effectively gave his guitar the quality of a mandolin. His presence on *Hotter than That*, a classic Hot Five recording with its

Lonnie Johnson, publicity photograph, 1920s.

broad, thrusting swing, was more of a revelation, in part because the tune was based harmonically not on the blues but on the dixieland favourite *Tiger Rag*, and thus demanded of Johnson something other than his usual riffs and routines. Accordingly, his counterpoint beneath Armstrong's 32-bar "scat" vocal improvisation — and somewhat obscured *by* it — hinted at the unfurling melodic line of jazz rather than emphasizing the reiterative melodic curl of the blues, the same curl to which Armstrong and Johnson immediately returned in the coy two-bar exchanges that followed, with Armstrong approximating vocally what Johnson played instrumentally.

Johnson was similarly inspired on his final side of consequence with Armstrong, *Mahogany Hall Stomp*, recorded in March 1929 by the trumpeter's Savoy Ballroom Five. Though the tune was once more a blues, it found Johnson in a particularly fanciful mood, one enhanced by the bright, ringing sound of his newly acquired 12-string guitar as he skipped lightly through a chorus on his own and then scampered for two more alongside Armstrong.

In the 15 months between his sessions with the Armstrong "Fives," Johnson recorded four tunes in New York in October and November 1928 with the Ellington orchestra, one of which, *Move Over*, was issued by OKeh as the work of "Lonnie Johnson's Harlem Footwarmers." Johnson's 12-string guitar added "a new luster," as Ellington put it,[25] to the orchestra's expanding palette of tones and textures; otherwise Johnson played much the same role with the Ellington orchestra as he had with Armstrong's bands. Again he was heard in solos and duets on three blues, *Move Over*, *The Mooche* and *Misty Mornin'*, and again he met the challenge of another *Tiger Rag* variant, *Hot and Bothered*, quite handily. His two choruses with the Chocolate

Dandies on yet another blues, *Paducah*, also recorded in the fall of 1928, were even more facile.

By then, OKeh had issued Johnson's own *Playing with the Strings* and *Stompin' em along Slow*, two remarkable guitar solos recorded the previous February in Memphis, the first piece at times almost frantic in its virtuosity and the second quite stinging in its intensity. These in turn set the stage for Johnson's influential duets with Eddie Lang, whose credits to that point had included a sojourn in London with the Mound City Blue Blowers and a remarkable series of recordings in New York with the violinist Joe Venuti.

Although Lang was as advanced a guitarist as any in jazz during the 1920s, he chose — or was asked by OKeh — to play a secondary role to Johnson's lead on each of their 10 duets from 1928 and 1929, all of them again blues, as were the two efficient sides that Lang, Johnson and others recorded as Blind Willie Dunn's Gin Bottle Four in 1929. Johnson's virtuosity was apparent once more in the duets — relaxed on *A Handful of Riffs*, brash on *Hot Fingers* — and clearly anticipated the directions that Teddy Bunn, Charlie Christian, Django Reinhardt and other jazz guitarists of the 1930s and 1940s would take.

Had Johnson never recorded again — had he done nothing else at all — his seminal contribution to both blues and jazz would nonetheless have been complete.

JOHNSON DID OF COURSE RECORD AGAIN, and often, although at intervals separated during the 1930s and 1950s by several years. And there was more to his career in the late 1920s, and long after, than just his recordings. He continued to work in and around St. Louis during the first years of his association with OKeh, a period in which Victoria Spivey remembered him "sitting on top of the piano playing violin with [his] brother James at Katey Red's in East St. Louis." Marvelled Spivey, "Dollar, five dollar and ten dollar bills would be flying as tips."[26] Another local musician, guitarist Henry Townsend, heard Johnson at the Booker Washington Theater and in speakeasies near Market Street and on 22nd Street in St. Louis and around 3rd Street across the river.[27]

Johnson's obligations to OKeh also took him farther afield. In the spring of 1928, for example, he visited San Antonio to record with Texas Alexander. He subsequently stopped for three weeks at the Ella B. Moore Theater in Dallas on his way back north. He also appeared in 1929 at several other TOBA theatres with Bessie Smith's troupe, the Midnite Steppers; to those "gals" he had boasted in *Roaming Rambler Blues* of having in Texas and Tennessee, he now added one more on tour — the Empress of the Blues herself. "She was sweet on me," Johnson suggested 30 years later, "but we never got real serious."[28]

Even in the immediate aftermath of the stock market crash in 1929, Johnson's prospects remained good. He continued to record frequently for OKeh — occasionally accompanying himself again at the piano — until the summer of 1932. But the Depression eventually took its toll on his career, as it did on so many other careers, leaving him to divide the rest of the 1930s in relative obscurity between Cleveland and Chicago, with periods of employment out of music in — according to one of his accounts — Galesburg and Peoria, Illinois.[29]

Back in Chicago, Johnson resumed his recording career with eight titles for Decca on his own in 1937 and eight more — from a session during a visit to New York — with a band in 1938. Having been ahead of his time stylistically in the mid-1920s, he sounded right up to date in the late 1930s; his unaccompanied instrumental *Swing out Rhythm*, which moved easily between blues and jazz, further revealed his skill as a guitarist to be undiminished. Another 33 sides followed under Johnson's name for Bluebird between 1939 and 1944, notably his hit *He's a Jelly Roll Baker*, which revived a sexual metaphor that he, among many other blues lyricists, had used successfully before.

Johnson was also busy again outside the recording studio. His versatility brought him work in Chicago with a fellow New Orleans musician, drummer Warren "Baby" Dodds, at the Three Deuces on North State Street — surely playing some jazz — and with the erstwhile St. Louis pianist Roosevelt Sykes at the Flame Club on South Indiana Avenue — just as surely playing the blues.

Nevertheless, the Chicago jazz magazine *Down Beat* acknowledged his presence in the city only incidentally during this period when it asked him in 1939 to contribute his recollections to a retrospective of Eddie Lang's career. Otherwise, Johnson — at the time working at the Three Deuces — was a largely overlooked figure, unable to attract even the 30 votes required that same year to tie Mike Pingatore, late of the Paul Whiteman Orchestra, for the 23rd and final place in the guitar category, won by Charlie Christian, of *Down Beat*'s annual Band Poll.[30]

Johnson described Lang, who had died in 1933 at the age of 30, as "the nicest man I ever worked with," and suggested that "he could play guitar better than anyone I know." But Johnson also alluded to his own turn of fortune when he spoke of the recordings that he and Lang had made together. "I valued those records more than anything in the world," he declared. "But one night not long ago, someone stole them from my house."[31]

Johnson remained in Chicago through the mid-1940s, making his last recordings for Aladdin there in June 1947 and his first of many for the King label in Cincinnati six months later. His initial King release, *Tomorrow Night*, billed as "Lonnie Johnson's Theme Song," was especially popular, holding No. 1 on *Billboard*'s Rhythm & Blues chart for seven weeks during the summer of 1948. His version of *Pleasing You (As Long as I Live)* was also a hit that year.[32] Together, the two songs signalled Johnson's new interest, after more than 30 years of blues, in singing ballads and popular material more generally — an interest, he later explained, that was as much pragmatic as anything else. "I have to do that in order to keep working," he admitted to the British journalist Valerie Wilmer, "'cause some places don't like the blues and then you don't have a job."[33]

At the same time, though, he maintained his ties to the past, joining trombonist Kid Ory, boogie-woogie pianist Jimmy Yancey and singers Estella "Mama" Yancey and Bertha "Chippie" Hill in the spring of 1948 for evenings of classic blues and jazz at Carnegie Hall in New York and Orchestra Hall in Chicago.[34]

He did not, however, maintain his ties to the Windy City. After the initial success of his recordings for King, he moved to Cincinnati, where he and his second wife, May, purchased an imposing three-storey house, complete with a two-storey turret, late in 1948. His association with King continued until mid-1952, by which point he had made more than 60 recordings. He lost his house a year later to foreclosure; whatever the financial return on the success of *Tomorrow Night* and his other King releases, and whatever the proceeds from a tour in England in 1952, he had apparently not made a payment on his mortgage in nearly three years.[35]

Johnson's fortunes continued to decline through the 1950s, his precise whereabouts uncertain during that period. According to the blues historian Samuel Charters, Johnson was still in Cincinnati as late as 1959; Charters, who characterized him as "a tall, thin, dark man, clumsy when he was not playing, often brooding and unhappy," repeated a second-hand report that he had been seen the year before while visiting Chicago, "a sick man, shabbily dressed."[36] But Chris Albertson, then an announcer on the Philadelphia radio station WHAT and later the biographer of Bessie Smith, "discovered" Johnson early in 1960 working locally as a janitor at the Benjamin Franklin Hotel, a position he had apparently held for "the past several years." As Johnson began his career anew with LPs for Bluesville, a reunion with Victoria Spivey and the first of many engagements that would take him across the United States, on to Europe and back to Canada, he appeared to Albertson in a very different light than he had to Charters.

"Lonnie, this lean man with a misleading, perpetually sad face," Albertson remembered, "looked much younger than his years."[37]

4. "Keys to the city"

When Lonnie Johnson stepped off the overnight bus from New York City at the Bay Street terminal in Toronto on June 21, 1965, he was met by an Englishman, John McHugh, owner of the Penny Farthing, and a Scotsman, Jim McHarg, whose Metro Stompers had been working for the past several Friday and Saturday nights at the Underground, in the Penny Farthing's basement.

McHugh and his wife Marilyn had opened the Penny Farthing in a semi-detached, three-storey Victorian home at 112 Yorkville Avenue in 1963. By 1965, after taking over the adjoining address to the east and combining the two houses, they were presenting music downstairs and on the main floor, and renting out rooms upstairs. They also operated two seasonal patios, one fronting on Yorkville Avenue and the other set around a swimming pool in the rear yard, where — weather permitting — patrons were served by waitresses in bikinis.

The Penny Farthing's music policy included folk, jazz, blues and even rock — the last albeit just fleetingly one May weekend in 1965 in the form of The Sparrows, a local band that went on to international success after moving via New York to the US west coast and reconstituting itself as Steppenwolf. Another performer at the Penny Farthing that month, the singer and songwriter Joni Mitchell, then performing as Joni Anderson, would take the same route to even greater fame. A third, guitarist Amos Garrett, was also just beginning his career when he appeared in early June as a member of a jug band known as the Dirty Shames; he, too, would emerge in due course as an influential figure stateside.[1]

Lonnie Johnson, on the other hand, was a long way from the start of *his* career, a point of fact that McHugh fully understood as he waited with Jim McHarg at the bus terminal. Both men were familiar with Johnson's story and loved his music, McHugh as a jazz fan of a dozen or more years' standing and McHarg as a musician whose career dated back to the early 1950s in Glasgow, where he had led the Clyde Valley Stompers in the revivalist "trad" style that was so popular throughout Great Britain. McHarg played banjo in those early years but had taken up string bass by the time he finally settled permanently in Toronto in 1963, after two shorter Canadian sojourns. The Metro Stompers were the second in the succession of dixieland bands that he would lead at jazz rooms, lounges and restaurants in and around the city during the next 40 years.

McHugh had not been among the few who had heard Johnson at the New Gate of Cleve in May 1965; his responsibilities at the Penny Farthing kept him from visiting other coffeehouses in the Village.[2] Instead, it was McHarg who convinced him to bring Johnson back to Toronto. "This hadn't been too difficult," McHarg wrote in a profile of Johnson that appeared a few months later in *Coda Magazine*, "as [McHugh] is a dyed-in-the-wool jazz fanatic and was enthusiastic about the project from the word go."

Still, they had some misgivings in anticipation of Johnson's return to Toronto. His first visit had not gone well and the outcome of his second, scarcely four weeks later, was at the very least uncertain. "How," McHarg remembered wondering, "would this sixty-year-old man, a star from another era, compete with blaring rock 'n roll, good-looking young folk singers and [the] phoney [sic] veneer that is discotheque. If my hunch was wrong, then it was going to cost someone some money and perhaps hurt a nice old man."

Johnson arrived on schedule, showing no ill effects from the long trip as he stepped down from the bus and collected his guitar and luggage. "Instead of meeting a tired old man as we expected," McHarg wrote, "the figure that confronted us was that of a sprightly fifty-year-old. His beaming smile and widely-set mischievous eyes instantly [dis]pelled all doubts I had been having."[3]

In their surprise and excitement, McHarg and McHugh found themselves offering Johnson a rather awestruck welcome. "It was like walking up and shaking hands with a page out of history," McHarg marvelled in a 1969 interview. "And we sort of didn't know what to say. But he chattered away at us and the first thing he asked was, 'How's the chick situation in Toronto?'"[4]

DAVID REA WAS IN THE HOUSE when Johnson opened at the Penny Farthing that same night, a Monday. Rea, just 18 and an exceptionally promising guitarist from a small town near Akron, Ohio, had moved to Toronto in the summer of 1964 at the suggestion of folksingers Ian and Sylvia, and was soon working in Yorkville coffeehouses as an accompanist to various other performers, including the Allen-Ward Trio and Gordon Lightfoot.

His memories of Johnson's opening set at the Penny Farthing remained vivid years later — the tuxedo that Johnson was wearing, set off by a red cummerbund, the cheap guitar that he played and especially the first song that he chose to sing, *I Left My Heart in San Francisco.*

Johnson's guitar was in fact a Kay electric of recent vintage, the Value Leader model, with a sunburst finish, a single pickup and a metal, checkerboard pickguard that ran like a racing stripe the length of its body. Johnson had personalized the instrument over time simply by playing it: the finish of the fifth, sixth, eighth and tenth frets of its maple fingerboard were worn dull where he had bent the guitar's upper strings to reach his favoured blue notes.

But there were no blue notes in *I Left My Heart in San Francisco*. Rea, who had read about Johnson in Samuel Charters' pioneering 1959 book *The Country Blues*, was not alone in his surprise at Johnson's decision to introduce himself at the Penny Farthing with a song that had recently been a Top 40 hit for Tony Bennett and that would come to serve Bennett as his signature for the rest of his career.

"The assembled blues and jazz cognoscenti were a little dumbfounded, to say the least," Rea mused. "It was like, well... have you ever seen an audience *im*plode? As I recall, someone said, 'Play *Tomorrow Night*.' He did, and of course the playing was brilliant. All of a sudden the audience changed, and he realized that people had come to see *him* and to hear *his* music. A big smile came over his face; it was a wonderful transformation."[5]

Johnson performed to a fair crowd that night, but by week's end was drawing full houses, thanks in part to word of mouth in Yorkville and in part to Patrick Scott's effusive review, with "Johnson deserves keys to city" as its headline, in Wednesday's *Globe and Mail.*

In this, the second of the many pieces that he would write about Johnson for the *Globe*, Scott once again set aside the appearance of critical objectivity, moving even beyond the role of advocate to that of apologist when — possibly in response to

John Norris' comments in the latest issue of *Coda Magazine* — he denounced "the tripe that some of the moldier figs around town are peddling to the effect that Johnson no longer can be classified as an authentic jazz musician because he is singing more love songs than he is blues; what are blues, may I ask[,] if they aren't in essence love songs?"

In his inventory of Johnson's opening-night performance, Scott itemized two generous sets, the first 75 minutes long and the second an hour, and an estimated minimum of 35 to 40 songs, ranging from Johnson's own *He's a Jelly Roll Baker* and two "utterly different" renditions of the classic *St. Louis Blues* to the pop songs *Blueberry Hill* and *Red Sails in the Sunset.*

"Don't take any pins," Scott advised, setting up a figurative allusion to the audience's response, "because you'll never hear them dropping." His final, unabashedly sentimental sentence provided his review with its headline. "If I were the mayor I would give him the keys to the city; as it is all I can offer is a personal, heartfelt wish: May he live and play and sing forever."[6]

This, from the same critic who took great sport, for example, in defying the esteem in which Oscar Peterson had been held by Toronto jazz fans, on one occasion admitting to "a childlike hope that one night [Peterson] will lose the key to his automatic piano and be forced to play it by hand again,"[7] and on another responding triumphantly to a reader's challenge that he make good on an assertion that he could name 25 other pianists he would rather hear — by naming 26.[8]

Scott's preferences in general tended either to older players in older styles or, on occasion, to younger players who had taken older styles to heart; he wrote enthusiastically in 1965 of pianists Don Ewell, Earl Hines, Sir Charles Thompson and Teddy Wilson, guitarist Marty Grosz and singers Olive Brown and Jimmy

Rushing, as well as the New York sextet known as the Saints and Sinners. Although he was favourably disposed toward modernist Thelonious Monk — "the only authentic giant, on any instrument, that [jazz] has produced in a quarter of a century"[9] — he treated Monk's fellow pianist Erroll Garner with complete disdain and declined even to review the clarinetists Buddy DeFranco and Jimmy Giuffre on the basis that they were simply not jazz musicians. "If he wants to call himself a jazz musician," Scott wrote of Giuffre, "that's his business, but I do not feel obligated to go on reporting, every time he turns up like a bad penny, that I think he stinks."[10]

Scott was not alone, however, in his glowing assessment of Lonnie Johnson. Sid Adilman, in attendance on behalf of both the Toronto *Telegram* and *Variety*, found Johnson at the Penny Farthing three nights later resplendent in a maroon sports jacket wide in the lapels, threadbare grey slacks and a red tie secured rather dangerously in place by "a stud almost as high as his chin."[11] Adilman began his *Telegram* review with a breathless proclamation — "Lonnie Johnson at 65 years of age outplays, outsings and outdraws the bulk of the hippy moderns" — and reported that this "outstanding talent" had "a full house whistling, shouting and stomping their feet for more."[12]

Frank Kennedy, reviewing Johnson the following week for Toronto's third major daily newspaper, the *Star*, made it unanimous. "I have always hesitated to use superlatives," he wrote, "[b]ut Wednesday night I had the warmest, most touching musical experience I have ever known. I heard a genius at work, a man who loves to sing, has given his life to it, and bares his heart and soul in song."[13]

Kennedy broached the apparent dichotomy in Johnson's repertoire, listing several of the songs that he heard that night, most of them pop standards — *I'm in the Mood for Love, Pennies from Heaven, I'm Confessin', It's a Sin to Tell a Lie, When You're Smiling, Rockin' Chair* and *September Song* — but concluding that Johnson was at his best "by far" when singing his own blues.

That sentiment was echoed a few days later in the *Telegram* by the paper's regular jazz columnist, Helen McNamara, always circumspect in her opinions and generally the "good cop" to Patrick Scott's "bad cop" on the Toronto jazz scene. "Much as we appreciated Mr. Johnson's considerable support of the popular song," she wrote, "the sound of his blues dwells longest. He is a man who knows unerringly how to extract their bitter truth."[14]

Between his pop material and his blues, Johnson sang until almost three a.m. on the occasion of Kennedy's visit. "He goes on for 80 or 90 songs a night," Kennedy reported. "Most singers think they're doing well with a dozen." In fact, the length of Johnson's performances had been a concern from his very first night at the Penny Farthing; he was asked almost immediately to limit his sets to 40 minutes, with another five for an encore, but rarely complied.

"His first set,"McHarg noted, harking back to opening night, "lasted an hour and ten minutes; we had expected the usual twenty minutes. Lonnie has no regard for time when people want to hear him sing... We devised a system where we were to stand in front of him so that he would know when it was time to come off. It didn't work too well. Every time John [McHugh] or I stood up, Lonnie just closed his eyes and went right on singing."[15]

Typically, he followed his own rules at the Penny Farthing. "I love to sing," he told Kennedy. "Some singers love payday. They sing for payday. I don't. I sing for you, for the people out there, for myself."[16] But if there was indeed a degree of self-absorption to the man, there was also the gentler grace of another era, a generosity largely untouched either by guile or by affectation.

"He remembered every waitress and dishwasher by name," McHarg wrote, "and did the rounds of the staff to greet them every evening before playing his first set. A young couple arrived just as he was going into his last number for the evening, and he finished up singing an extra fifteen minutes just for them."[17]

Moreover, Johnson's agreement with the Penny Farthing called for him to do a few numbers downstairs late on Friday and Saturday nights with the Metro Stompers — McHarg and his fellow Scotsman Charlie Gall, a cornetist in the direct and forceful style of Muggsy Spanier, as well as the Danish clarinetist Eric Nielson and two Englishmen, banjo player Ron Simpson and drummer Bernie Nathan. Theirs was "a union made in heaven," pronounced Patrick Scott, who dropped by on a particularly hot and humid Friday evening in early July. He was particularly taken with their version of *St. Louis Blues*, which "generated more electricity than the thunderstorm outside."[18]

Adding the role of publicist to that of apologist, Scott also took note of the latest developments: after only two weeks in town, Johnson had already lined up his next engagement — at Steele's Tavern on Yonge Street. And there was talk of a recording session with Don Ewell, still in residence at the Golden Nugget.[19]

5. "The stretch of it"

Charlie Gall and Lonnie Johnson had two things in common — three including praise from Patrick Scott, who deemed the Glaswegian cornetist "Scotland's greatest gift to jazz since Eddie Condon was introduced to Chivas Regal," a reference to the hard-drinking New York guitarist who recognized a good Scotch whiskey when he tasted it.[1]

Gall and Johnson were both new to Toronto in 1965 and each had known Louis Armstrong. Gall was the first to arrive in the city, after several years on the "trad" scene in London and — before London — in Glasgow, where he had been a member of the Clyde Valley Stompers, post-Jim McHarg, when they opened for Armstrong's All Stars at Kelvin Hall in 1956.

Charlie Gall and Louis Armstrong, Kelvin Hall, Glasgow, 1956. Courtesy Charlie Gall.

A photograph from that evening caught Gall and Armstrong standing shoulder-to-shoulder in a serious moment together backstage: Gall, 21 and looking much younger, cornet held lightly, left ear cocked attentively in Armstrong's direction; Armstrong, 54, trumpet and white handkerchief at the ready, right hand raised conspiratorially to his mouth, masking their conversation.

Gall and Armstrong had blown a few notes together in Armstrong's dressing room but mostly they talked — about embouchure, about the acoustics of Kelvin Hall and, at one point, about a potentially embarrassing situation for the Stompers.

"We had a singer by the name of Mary McGowan," Gall recalled. "She wasn't really a jazz singer but she could belt out *Bill Bailey*, you know? Of course Louis had Velma Middleton with him. And [his manager] Joe Glaser said, 'Louis already has a female singer; your singer can't perform.' Mary was terribly upset: it was a big occasion, she'd got a nice new dress. I mentioned this to Louis. He said, 'Stay here.' Away he went to talk to Joe Glaser, and when he came back he said, 'Charlie, the canary sings.'"

Gall would tell that story again and again over the years; he may well have repeated it to Johnson. The two men certainly spoke of their mutual friend, although Gall remembered that Johnson had little to say about Armstrong — or about any other subject, for that matter.

"When I first met Lonnie I was struck by how unassuming and humble a man he was. I think he had been so busy all his life, trying to make a living, that he had no pretensions. He didn't discuss his private life at all; he didn't even mention much about Louis. I asked him; I told him I'd met Louis, that I'd done the concert with Louis. He just smiled and said, 'A great man.' That was about the stretch of it."[2]

6. "Two old warriors"

Lonnie Johnson was still at the Penny Farthing when Louis Armstrong himself opened for a week at O'Keefe Centre on July 19, 1965. Johnson stopped by one night for a visit backstage, accompanied by Jim McHarg. "Hadn't seen him since the Twenties when we made those records together," Armstrong told Patrick Scott a few days later. "He was doing me a favor to record with me then. Sure nice to hear he's makin' out good up here."[1]

The O'Keefe Centre engagement — six shows in a hall seating 3,200 — was a measure of Armstrong's standing not just in jazz by 1965 but in popular music more generally. He had made his mark during the 1920s with his Hot Five and Hot Seven recordings, redefining jazz as a soloist's art and setting that art's enduring standards for invention, technique and risk. With his place in the history of jazz assured, he began in the 1930s to redefine himself, or *allow* himself to be redefined, now as an entertainer for whom the trumpet was but one element of several — among them an endearingly coarse singing voice — in a stage persona that appealed to a far wider audience than he would ever have reached on his instrumental skill alone. His recording of *Hello Dolly*, for example, broke a 14-week run of Beatles songs atop the *Billboard* singles chart in May 1964.

Armstrong reprised *Hello Dolly* no less than six times with his All Stars on opening night at O'Keefe Centre; he also sang *Mack the Knife* and *Blueberry Hill*, two of his lesser pop hits from the mid-1950s, and even played *My Country 'Tis of Thee*,

Louis Armstrong and Lonnie Johnson, O'Keefe Centre, Toronto, July 1965.
Photograph by Jim McHarg. Courtesy Charlie Gall.

which shared its melody with *God Save the Queen*, the anthem then customarily performed at the start of public events in Toronto. But he offered just one tune, *Struttin' with Some Barbeque*, to stand for the legacy of his Hot Five and Hot Seven recordings 30 years earlier — the legacy to which Lonnie Johnson had in a small way contributed, evidently as a favour.

The headlines in Toronto's newspapers on July 20 were reserved but respectful: "Same old Satchmo but fans love it" (*Telegram*), "Satchmo has flashes of brilliance" (*Star*) and "A lean performance from Louis" (*Globe and Mail*).[2] But given time to reflect on what he had heard, Patrick Scott offered a longer and rather more severe assessment that appeared in the *Globe* on the final day of the engagement.

Armstrong at 63 was, in Scott's words, "captive to this burning desire to die with his valves down" — that is, to go out swinging. But his determination in that regard, admirable though it may have been, was taking its toll. "He smiled his trademark smile (and rolled his eyes and shook his jowls and brandished his handkerchiefs) when the occasion demanded," Scott wrote, "but he spent much more of his time — right there on the stage, in front of all those people! — slump-shouldered against the piano, staring somberly at his shoes, or off into space."

Gone from Armstrong's performance, Scott suggested, was its element of risk; gone, much of its ebullience. "He can still chill the spine, even when not taking chances, but the fact remains that the most inventive performer that jazz has ever known, the most imitated instrumentalist it has ever produced, now is content to imitate the shadow of himself."[3]

Thus the view from the aisle. Backstage, where Armstrong received Johnson and McHarg warmly in his dressing room, the scene was no less poignant. McHarg had met Armstrong a few times before, but not *this* Armstrong.

"The man talking to Lonnie Johnson was a different person entirely," McHarg wrote in his profile of Johnson for *Coda Magazine*. "Absent was the big grin, the flashing teeth and the popping eyeballs. In their place was registered the genuine pleasure of seeing an old friend. An air of sadness prevailed in the dressing room as the two old warriors talked of their families and friends and recaptured memories of youthful days in their beloved New Orleans. This wasn't the King of Jazz giving an audience to one of his poor subjects. Rather, it was a meeting of two tired souls who[,] after giving everything they had to jazz, were searching each others [sic] face to find out if it had all been worth while."[4]

7. "The picture of sophistication"

Lonnie Johnson made friends quickly and easily in Toronto, beginning with the members of the Metro Stompers. He visited Bernie Nathan and his wife occasionally for dinner at their home on Dupont Street; duly charmed by their guest, the Nathans named their first born son in his honour. Johnson also joined other Stompers and their wives on day trips to Musselman Lake, a popular resort spot northeast of Toronto. And, as he had with Patrick Scott, he brought out the best in Jim McHarg, otherwise an intense and at times difficult character on the Toronto jazz scene.

The Metro Stompers (left to right): Jim McHarg, Charlie Gall, Ron Simpson, Eric Nielson, Bernie Nathan, Toronto, 1965. Courtesy Charlie Gall.

Yet another of the Stompers came to Johnson's professional assistance. Charlie Gall, who had taken a job with the performing rights organization Broadcast Music Inc. (BMI) Canada upon his arrival in Toronto, was surprised to learn that Johnson was a member in the United States neither of BMI nor of its rival, ASCAP — the American Society of Composers, Authors and Publishers. "No one," Gall recalled, "had ever pointed him in any particular direction." Johnson had long since lost control of his old songs, but he was able to register his newer ones with BMI Canada, among them *Brenda*, an ode to the infant daughter he had left in Philadelphia.

Beyond the Stompers, Johnson also made the acquaintance of two musicians from the Black Eagle Jazz Band, cornetist Joe van Rossem and banjo player Cliff Bastin, who were renting adjacent rooms on the second floor of the Penny Farthing; the Black Eagles had worked in the club's basement on occasion in 1964. Like the members of the Stompers, van Rossem and Bastin were recent to Canada, the former arriving from Holland in 1958 and the latter from England in 1962; Bastin would eventually switch to trumpet and, as Kid Bastien, led a succession of rough and ready New Orleans-styled bands at Grossman's Tavern on Spadina Avenue until his death in 2003.

Johnson visited van Rossem and Bastin on occasion during his engagements at the Penny Farthing; van Rossem remembered him as "a very gentle, slight man, a wonderful guy to be around," though not — as Charlie Gall had also discovered — especially forthcoming about his early years. "I talked to him about the old days — those recordings with Louis. Didn't get much out of that. Later on I met Louis' wife, Lil. She was like that too."[1]

With his room more or less directly above the stage downstairs on the main floor, van Rossem heard Johnson nightly and came to know his repertoire of ballads and blues well, perhaps *too* well — well enough, in any event, to be able to play it himself, as in fact he did one evening. "I recall being kind of fed up with it," he admitted, referring to the repetition of songs. "I knew everything he always did. I just went down with my cornet and played with him. He didn't mind at all."

Out on Yorkville Avenue, Johnson inevitably attracted attention as an African-American of a certain age among the Village's young, white hippies. The press that he received during his first run at the Penny Farthing would have quickly made him something of a local celebrity.

"He had a big entourage of mostly young guitarists," remembered one of their number, Leigh Cline, who played in a finger-picked, folk-blues style. The two men once shared a Toronto Folk Music Guild workshop with Amos Garrett; after Cline had demonstrated his style, Johnson turned to him and said, "Boy, I wish I could play like that." Years later, Cline was still amazed by the comment. "*He's* telling *me*, 'I wish I could play like that.' He was so supportive."[2]

Of course not everyone in the Village quite knew who Johnson was. "I was walking down Yorkville with him one day, having a nice chat," recounted the Stompers' Ron Simpson, "when he came across a hippie with a guitar like a bow." A guitar, that is, with extremely "high" action, in which the strings are set at some distance from the fingerboard; the higher the strings, the louder the guitar, but also the harder to play.

"Lonnie said, 'Hey, give me that thing, boy.' So the kid gave him the guitar. Lonnie knocked out a fantastic blues, gave the guitar back and left the kid standing there with his mouth wide open."[3]

JOHNSON'S NEW CIRCLE OF FRIENDS broadened beyond Yorkville when he was invited on one of his days off in August to a house party in suburban Don Mills, where he was entertained by Tubby Fats' Original All Star Downtown Syncopated Big Rock Jug Band, a group of teenagers from Don Mills Collegiate, among them the Whiteley brothers, Chris and Ken.[4]

Chris, 17, played harmonica and guitar; Ken, 14, jug and banjo. Both would emerge in the 1980s as significant figures among Canada's "roots" musicians, but for the moment they were caught up in the folk revival of the 1960s — the same folk revival that had given new impetus to Johnson's career.

"We went fairly quickly from hearing Peter, Paul and Mary and the Kingston Trio on the radio, on CHUM or whatever," Ken recalled, "to discovering Sam the Record Man, where John Norris worked. He would say, 'Well, if you like *that*, you should check *this* out.' We got a lot of great records from him."[5]

Indeed the Whiteleys soon found their way from the revivalist Jim Kweskin, Dave Van Ronk and Even Dozen jug bands of the early 1960s back to the Memphis Jug Band, Gus Cannon's Jug Stompers and Clarence Williams' Jug Band of the 1920s and 1930s — and from there to other blues, jazz and even country artists of that early, classic era.

As it happened, Johnson had recorded with one of Williams' jug bands for OKeh in 1930. And now, 35 years later, he was in Toronto. "Here," Ken suggested, "was a living connection to blues and jazz from the 1920s and 1930s."

The Whiteleys and the three other members of the Tubby Fats band — Tom Evans, who played mandolin and violin, and the Lee brothers, Michael and Patrick, who handled gutbucket and washboard, respectively — spent some of the summer of 1965 working in the Muskoka town of Bracebridge, north of

Toronto. They were home in mid-August, however, when Evans' mother, serving as the band's manager, invited Johnson, Jim McHarg, Patrick Scott, the Dirty Shames and a select few others over for the evening. Johnson, who arrived with a young woman on his arm, sang and played for the small audience in the Evans' candle-lit recreation room,[6] and listened as young Tom, the Whiteleys and the Lees offered a few songs of their own.

"We were nervous to play before a legend," Chris Whiteley remembered, "but he was extremely gracious and complimentary and encouraging. He took the time to speak with us."[7] One of their songs was *Brown's Ferry Blues*, originally recorded in 1933 by two white musicians from Alabama, the Delmore Brothers, who played and sang the blues in an oldtime country style. "I think it kind of tickled Lonnie that we were into this music that he had devoted his life to. He really seemed to get a genuine kick out of it."

Johnson offered Chris Whiteley in particular a memorable word of advice. "He looked at my guitar, played it a little and said, 'You should raise the action.' I've favoured a high action ever since."

Whenever the Whiteleys saw Johnson again — in Yorkville and, later, in other Toronto nightspots — he would always nod from the stage and go over to say hello on the break, cutting quite the dapper figure in their young eyes with the suits that he wore, the holder that he used with his cigarettes and, of course, the female company that he kept. "To me at the time," Chris marvelled, "he was just the picture of sophistication."

The Whiteleys and their friends in turn made an impression of their own on Johnson. After that evening in Don Mills, Jim McHarg later wrote, "[Lonnie] enthused to me about their playing all the way back to the hotel."[8]

8. "Olives akimbo"

Lonnie Johnson closed on July 24 at the Penny Farthing and opened on August 16 downtown at Steele's Tavern on Yonge Street, one door north of Sam the Record Man and one door south of Sam Sniderman's main competition, A&A Records. Johnson was something of a departure from the tavern's usual fare of young, white troubadours, among them in 1965 Gordon Lightfoot, Tom Shipley, Klaas Van Graft and Alan McRae, all of whom either sang their own songs or drew on American and British folk traditions.

They, too, had worked in Yorkville coffeehouses. But, as they, and Johnson, quickly discovered, Yorkville Avenue was quite different than Yonge Street, one of the city's main retail thoroughfares, lined with banks, restaurants, taverns, movie houses, furniture stores and men's fashion shops. The prevalent sound there was rhythm and blues, as heard at the Club Bluenote, across the street and a block to the north from Steele's Tavern; the prevalent attitude was a workaday sort of pragmatism, hardened by the same realities of money and power that Yorkville's hippies, in their idealism, had sought to escape.

And yet Johnson's reception there, according to Patrick Scott, who was dutifully present on opening night, seemed no different than it had been at the Penny Farthing. "He was not halfway through his opening theme, *When You're Smiling,*" Scott wrote in *The Globe and Mail,* "before the bartender in the upstairs lounge at Steele's Tavern had deserted both his customers and his cash register to stand transfixed, as though nailed to the floor, applauding an artist. And the customers, as far as I could detect, could not have cared less, because they, too — swizzle sticks frozen in mid-air, olives akimbo — hung on every note."

Scott acknowledged the dissimilarities between Yorkville and Yonge Street, but suggested that everything else — the songs Johnson sang and the response they generated — remained the same. Noting the many requests that Johnson had received on his first night, Scott added agreeably, "My own favorite Lonnie Johnson number happens to be the one he is singing or playing at any given time."[1]

Things had apparently changed before Frank Kennedy dropped by just three nights later to update his regular Saturday column in the *Star*. He, too, recalled Johnson's performances at the Penny Farthing, where "night after night for weeks [he] topped the performance of the night before." And he, too, remembered the audience's undivided attention there.

Not so now. "I found it difficult to give Lonnie an honest hearing," he admitted. "Throughout the performance, there was a buzz of conversation throughout the room. Worst offenders were two men who I had the misfortune to be sitting next to at the bar. The main difference, I suppose, is that the Penny Farthing patrons went first of all to hear Lonnie. The Steele's customers went primarily to have a drink."[2]

Kennedy returned to the subject a few weeks later in a review of Alan McRae, observing, on the basis of recent visits to Steele's Tavern, that "the paying customers have shown little regard for the performer" and continued, "[t]his same problem bothered Lonnie Johnson during his stay there, and definitely impaired his usually top-level performance."[3]

Still, the engagement was expected to last only two weeks. And, as Scott reported, Johnson had at least four other clubs bidding for his services. "I would not be at all surprised," Scott mused hopefully, "if he is in Toronto to stay."[4]

9. "Nobody loved music"

First Louis, then Lil — Lil Hardin Armstrong, Louis' second wife and the pianist on most of his classic Hot Five and Hot Seven sides, including those from 1927 with Lonnie Johnson. A month after Louis spent a week at O'Keefe Centre, Lil arrived in Toronto for three at the Penny Farthing and was held over for a fourth. A reunion of some sort with Johnson would have been natural. He, however, had left town immediately after his engagement at Steele's Tavern.

"I went to this other place out there somewhere and I want to forget all about it forever," Johnson recalled quite vaguely late the following year, by then having in fact pretty much forgotten about it altogether. "The place was filled every night and nobody loved music, and I have played to audiences that listen. All you could hear was people saying, 'Bring me another drink.' Oh, I couldn't please anyone there. The place had three syllables, and I'll remember it in a — OTTAWA! That's it. Ottawa. The most miserable time, I liked to [have] died."[1]

The Belle Claire Hotel on Queen Street was a colourful Ottawa establishment popular with politicians, sports figures and other characters of like or lesser repute. There was no cover charge in the Belle Claire's Celebrity Lounge, where Johnson appeared throughout September 1965, but there was certainly a clamour, more so apparently than even at Steele's Tavern. For once, Johnson wasn't exaggerating; instead he left out an important twist in the story.

"When one end of the long, angled room got noisy," reported "Gard." in *Variety,* after dropping by the Belle Claire on September 21, "Johnson quietly left [the] stage and mike, turned his back and sang conclusively to the other end. It worked like magic: the far end piped down to hear what was going on and stayed mum when, after two floor numbers, he stepped back up to close the 40-minute set with a highly individualized 'When You're Smiling.'"[2]

10. "The best Canadian jazz LP of all time"

Lonnie Johnson spent the next five months, October 1965 through February 1966, alternating between return visits to the Penny Farthing and to Steele's Tavern — between adulation and, from one night to the next, degrees of indifference. He was in the midst of an extended run at the Yonge Street nightspot when he and the Metro Stompers met at the behest of Columbia Records on November 24, a Wednesday, in the RCA recording studio on Mutual Street. Johnson had made hundreds of recordings by then; the Stompers, just one — an audition tape done a few weeks earlier with CJRT-FM announcer Ted O'Reilly in a TV studio at the Ryerson Institute of Technology, a tape made in order to give Columbia an idea of how well the band might fare away from the Penny Farthing, where the clamour of an appreciative audience masked any deficiencies that the musicians may have had. Evidently the band fared well enough.

Patrick Scott was of course present in the studio on the 24th, accompanied on this occasion by his 11-year-old son. John Norris was also on hand, although he — unlike Scott, who had attached himself unreservedly to Johnson by then — was not one of the American's confidants. "I was ambivalent about what he was doing musically at that time," Norris explained years later, referring in particular to the pop songs that Johnson chose to sing. "It wouldn't have been really honest to be his friend and not be enthusiastic about what he was doing."[1]

The Columbia initiative nevertheless warranted Norris' attention as the editor of *Coda Magazine*, so few and far between were jazz recording sessions for commercial labels in Canada during the early 1960s. The Hallmark, London and RCA Victor labels had made dixieland LPs with the Toronto cornetist Trump Davidson, Edmonton's Tailgate Jazz Band and the Vancouver clarinetist Lance Harrison, respectively; RCA had also recorded a few modernists, notably the Montreal saxophonist Nick Ayoub and two Toronto musicians, pianist Brian Browne and clarinetist Phil Nimmons, the latter with his tentet, Nimmons 'n' Nine. Not until 1968, however, when Norris established Sackville Records with Bill Smith — by then his partner at *Coda Magazine* — and others, did the recording of jazz in Canada really begin in earnest.

According to Norris' report in the December 1965 issue of *Coda Magazine*, the Metro Stompers recorded a total of 16 tunes at the Columbia session. All but three were issued on the LP *Stompin' at the Penny*, including six that featured Johnson. He sang on three: his own *Mr. Blues Walks* and *Bring It on Home to Mama*, as well as the most sentimental of the ballads in his repertoire, *My Mother's Eyes*. He also played three instrumentals, including *China Boy* and *West End Blues*, each a classic of the traditional jazz repertoire on the basis of recordings, respectively, by Red McKenzie, Eddie Condon and their Chicagoans in 1927 and by Louis Armstrong in 1928. Johnson made up the third instrumental, *Go Go Swing*, in the studio.

In fact most of his tracks with the Stompers had a casually extemporized quality. Johnson sang and played as he might have if he were on his own, and the band found its way alongside, Jim McHarg, Ron Simpson and Bernie Nathan offering basic rhythmic support, and Charlie Gall and Eric Nielson alternating or combining with Johnson on obbligatos.

As Nathan remembered it, the Stompers' lack of recording experience was at first plainly evident. "We couldn't get anything straight," the drummer explained, "so we took a break. Someone went to the LCBO [Liquor Control Board of Ontario] and came back with a jug. We got into that, started again and it was okay."[2]

Johnson kept his thoughts to himself while the band dealt with the "cracked notes, bent smiles and broken tempos" that Patrick Scott identified as "noticeable signs of 'studio jitters'" in his liner notes to the LP.[3]

"Lonnie was great at the session," Gall remembered. "He was very quiet, he never offered any directions or instructions, all he asked was just, 'What are we going to do with *My Mother's Eyes*?' We talked it over, and we did it."

Johnson's concern about the presentation of *My Mother's Eyes*, and the fact that he even wished to record such a prim song with the Stompers, reflected the personal significance that he had attached to it. In the event — after he and the band had recorded their three instrumentals together — he gave *My Mother's Eyes* a sweet, plaintive reading, quite unlike his commanding version of *Bring It on Home to Mama*, which he worked up almost to a shout, and his weary interpretation of *Mr. Blues Walks*, which fell somewhere between resignation and despondence. He also put his guitar aside for *My Mother's Eyes* — the better to drop to one knee, figuratively speaking, and, with arms wide, reach for the song's cadential high note on the final "my" before resolving it on "mother's eyes" and adding a satisfied "Oh yeah" as a gentle two-note coda.

If *My Mother's Eyes* was on several counts the session's anomaly, then *West End Blues* was its revelation, no matter Gall's wavering attempt to replicate the remarkable opening proclamation that Louis Armstrong had recorded 37 years earlier. The Scotsman started jauntily enough but seemed after the first phrase to think better of the challenges that lay ahead and took evasive action instead. He did so rather elegantly, but in later years remained embarrassed at the recollection. "All I was really trying to do," he explained, "was give a nod of the head to Louis' famous introduction. Later on, I was able to play it all, but in those days I only had a smattering of it."

A smattering was nevertheless sufficient to introduce the first of Johnson's two impressive solos, a stinging double chorus whose insistent lines and figures seemed all the more urgent for the tune's slow tempo and the Stompers' processional accompaniment. His second solo was a shade more measured, both in length — just a single chorus — and in design, but no less inspired.

By contrast, his solos over the rousing swing of *China Boy* and the fast shuffle of *Go Go Swing* were a twangy pastiche of blues riffs, licks and clichés, many of them in fact his own, some dating as far back as his recordings with Eddie Lang 36 years earlier, but in total the work of someone who would seem to have followed the great figures in blues and jazz guitar rather than of someone who had led them.

All the same, John Norris and Patrick Scott were in agreement about the session's considerable value, although each writer expressed himself in character. Norris suggested with typical reserve that "unless something terrible happens to the music between tape and disc it should be something well worth while."[4] Scott announced that the recording "could be (provided Columbia's engineers did their job as well as the musicians) the best Canadian jazz LP of all time."[5] On the occasion of the LP's release in early February 1966, he harked back to his earlier prediction and proclaimed, "Well, they did, and it is."[6]

Scott acknowledged his own contribution to the LP only coyly in his review for *The Globe and Mail* by noting that his lone criticism of the album was the extent to which the liner notes, "by a Toronto jazz columnist with the initials P.S.," had been changed. Such a clear conflict of interest did not restrain him from promoting the LP to his readers, commending Johnson and Charlie Gall in particular and praising the album in general; *Stompin' at the Penny*, he suggested, was destined to be a collector's item, not least for the "full, limitless range of Johnson's singing skills."[7]

John Norris, meanwhile, sought out a more impartial opinion for *Coda Magazine*, assigning its review to an American writer, Wayne Jones, the drummer with a popular Chicago traditional jazz band, the Salty Dogs. Jones was predictably less impressed by the recording than Patrick Scott had been, suggesting that Johnson's "singing and playing are really the only things that lift it above the millrun." While Jones described the Stompers as being "well-rehearsed and tight" and singled out Charlie Gall and Eric Nielson as "excellent players," he also took note of the band's various lapses in technique and taste before concluding rather philosophically, "Lonnie has better albums available, and perhaps, in time, Jim McHarg will too."[8]

11. "Brownie was after him"

Jackie Washington was not strictly a blues musician. The genial Hamilton singer and guitarist did a little of everything, drawing on a repertoire of pop songs, novelties and jazz tunes that ran into the hundreds and eventually topped a thousand. But Washington was black and, as such, saw himself annexed more or less by default to the folk-music revival of the 1960s as the lone Canadian counterpart to Son House, Skip James and the other veteran African-American bluesmen who had recently been reclaimed from obscurity.

Washington's professional career dated back to the 1930s, when he and three of his brothers took the Mills Brothers as their model and sang as The Washingtons in dance halls around southern Ontario. Washington himself also worked for the Canadian Pacific Railroad — Oscar Peterson's father, Daniel, was a fellow porter — and spent time in the late 1940s as a disc-jockey at the Hamilton radio station CHML. He never stopped performing, though, and when the 1960s presented him with new opportunities as a musician, he was ready.

Some of those opportunities took him to Yorkville — to the Penny Farthing, for example, where he stopped by one night with his guitar on an impromptu coffeehouse crawl. "They got me up to play," he recalled, "and I played a few of my songs, which they didn't know. When I finished I went on to another place and the audience followed me."

Such was Washington's profile in the Village by late 1965 that he found himself invited to participate in a matinee on December 19 at the Riverboat with Lonnie Johnson and the popular duo of Sonny Terry and Brownie McGhee, whose 20 years in New York had scarcely tempered their spirited "Piedmont" style of country blues at all.

"Each one of us had to come out and do a couple of numbers on the guitar," Washington remembered. "Brownie was first. He played a couple of numbers on guitar, then he went over to the piano. Sonny had a harmonica for just about every key. So he said, 'What key ya in, Brownie?'

"Brownie said, 'I'm in the key of C.'

"Sonny said, 'Okay, I gotcha.' He had a harmonica for that.

"Then Lonnie came out, and he played a couple of numbers on guitar, then went over to the piano.

"Sonny said the same thing: 'What key ya in, Lonnie?'

"Lonnie said, 'I'm in B-flat.'

"Sonny said, 'Okay, I gotcha.'

"Now it was my turn. I come out and played a couple of numbers, then went over to the piano.

"Sonny said, 'What key ya in, Jackie?'

"I said, '*D*-flat.'

"Sonny said, 'Good *gawd*!'"

Washington recalled that he sang *Lovin' Mama Blues* and *Jelly, Jelly*, songs originally recorded in the years around 1940 by Joe Turner and Billy Eckstine, respectively. He also performed his own *Everyday Blues*. But in reality, he no more limited himself to the blues than did Johnson.

In fact, Johnson's penchant for singing ballads had raised McGhee's ire at the Riverboat. "Brownie was after him to stick to the blues," Washington mused. "I don't know if Lonnie was in love, or what, but he was playing love songs. And Brownie didn't approve."

The subject came up over a couple of bottles of Scotch backstage. "Brownie said that Lonnie's thing was really the blues, that Lonnie could play anything, but he was best on the blues. They had a heated argument about that. God, it was funny."[1]

Johnson would encounter similar responses from some of the other blues musicians who visited Toronto in the late 1960s. "He'd want to sit in with them," remembered his friend and manager Roberta Richards (later Barrett), who also booked Bukka White, Blind John Davis and Roosevelt Sykes for local appearances during this period, "and yet they didn't really want to play with him any longer, because it was almost as though he'd left the ranks and moved up."[2]

Still, Johnson's differences with McGhee at the Riverboat didn't stop him from revisiting one of his earliest recorded songs, *Falling Rain Blues*, with McGhee in John Arnold's place at the piano. It was, according to John Dafoe of *The Globe and Mail*, "the finest performance of the afternoon."[3]

12. *The Blues*

Sonny Terry and Brownie McGhee made a quick return to Toronto to participate in the filming on January 27, 28 and 29, 1966, of a historic blues special for the CBC-TV series *Festival* — historic, in view of the musicians assembled by its producer and director, Paddy Sampson.

Muddy Waters and his band — with pianist Otis Spann, harmonica player James Cotton and others — were on hand, as were the bassist and songwriter Willie Dixon and the pianist Sunnyland Slim, all of them luminaries of post-war, urban Chicago blues. Sonny Terry and Brownie McGhee, as well as Jesse "Lone Cat" Fuller, Bukka White and Big Joe Williams, represented the older, country blues styles of the south, while Mable Hillary from St. Simon Island, Georgia, stood in for all of the women who had so successfully followed Mamie Smith's lead with *Crazy Blues* in 1920. The Texan Lightnin' Hopkins had also been invited but, with a glance at both the calendar and a map, thought better of travelling anywhere when and where there might be snow.[1]

There were 15 performers altogether, assembled in a variety of combinations against the "night sky" of a dark, starlit backdrop on an otherwise bare soundstage at the CBC's Mutual Street studio.[2] The Toronto jazz drummer Archie Alleyne was one of the 15 — he accompanied Sunnyland Slim and Mable Hillary — but remarkably, Lonnie Johnson, working nightly just a five-minute walk away on Yonge Street, was not.

Remarkably and *inexplicably*. Unless Johnson's loyalty to Steele's Tavern kept him from accepting an offer that might have created a conflict in his schedule. Unless Johnson's presence in Toronto was not known to the American agent who booked the other musicians for Paddy Sampson. Or unless Johnson's blues, and especially his pop songs, were deemed in their sentimentality and relative sophistication to be lacking the fundamental qualities that characterized the music that Muddy Waters, Bukka White and the others played and that Sampson evidently valued, given the absence as well from the show of any stylish, younger Chicago musicians — a Buddy Guy, for example, or an Otis Rush.

Perhaps Johnson *had* been asked and, for reasons known only to himself, simply said, "No, thank you." By nature, he was quietly, though resolutely disinclined to serve to anyone's purposes but his own, especially if it meant conforming to someone else's ideal of the music that he had played for the past 50 years. "I wouldn't change my style for no one," he told Valerie Wilmer while touring Europe in 1963 with some of these same musicians — Waters, Willie Dixon, Otis Spann and Big Joe Williams. "I'm not a country blues singer and I don't intend to be one."[3]

Whatever the explanation for Johnson's absence from such an illustrious group of blues musicians in Toronto, whether personal or professional, it coincided with a downturn in his fortunes around town more generally. He was then in the last week of what proved to be his final run at Steele's Tavern. His next engagement took him full circle to the New Gate of Cleve, though just for two weeks.[4] And by the time the CBC televised part one of *The Blues* on February 23, 1966, he had just started his last engagement at the Penny Farthing.

There would be no reunion with the Metro Stompers there; Jim McHarg had taken the band from the basement of the Penny Farthing to the basement of Le Coq d'Or, a Yonge Street bar a few doors south of Steele's Tavern. Nor did the release of *Stompin' at the Penny* a few weeks earlier have any effect on Johnson's prospects — either with or without the Stompers. By early March, he was at loose ends for the first time in the eight months that he had spent in Toronto.

13. "Sing all night, if I want to"

Lonnie Johnson was back on Yorkville Avenue. In what the Toronto *Star* described as "a $7,000 gamble," taking Johnson at his word on the size of the risk involved, he opened his own club almost directly across the street from the Penny Farthing on the former premises of another coffeehouse, the Left Bank, at 107. The Home of the Blues he called it, and in short order he proved the name prophetic.

Johnson had owned a club once before, in St. Louis during the early 1930s, or so he told the *Star*, which took him at his word on that as well. "It was called Lonnie's Hideout," he declared. "It kept open for 14 years and I hope I make it as long this time."

In fact the Home of the Blues, which was launched with a private party on May 4, 1966, made it to six weeks, perhaps seven. Not that it was an entirely unreasonable idea; Johnson, after all, had become something of a celebrity during his 10 months in the city. "Toronto people went for me big," he boasted to the *Star*, harking back to his reception at the Penny Farthing during the previous summer. "I found I was able to earn $400 a week on average."

While he could have had no expectations of doing that well at the Home of the Blues — if in truth he had done that well elsewhere in Yorkville — he was looking forward to being his own boss. "No waiter'll serve drinks when I'm singing," he promised, the din at Steele's Tavern and the Celebrity Lounge of Ottawa's Belle Claire Hotel apparently still ringing in his ears.

"This place is going to be different. It's going to be friendly, really friendly. At my time of life that's really important to me."

Whether Johnson was truly feeling the vulnerability of his years just then, or simply playing for sympathy, he made a second allusion to his seniority when he spoke of the modest weekly rent — $50 — that he was apparently paying for the room. "That means I'll be able to stay a long, long time. That sure is a comfort to me, at my age."

He reiterated both his intentions and his sudden concern with mortality to the *Star* after his first set on opening night. "Gee," he enthused, "this is great. No one to give me the nod when to stop or start. I can really give, give, give to my audience. Sing all night, if I want to... For a guy pushing 70, like me, this is so important. I really feel at home."[1]

But the Home of the Blues was tiny, a basement room where — in Patrick Scott's words — "20 patrons make a crowd."[2]

Lonnie Johnson at the Home of the Blues, Toronto, May 1966. Photograph by James Lewcun. Courtesy *The Globe and Mail.*

Johnson was able to perform unamplified, but with admission at $1.50, which included a cup of coffee and the offer of a refill for just 50 cents more,[3] the club's nightly revenue stream was extremely, and unsustainably, limited.

"It never did very well," remembered the young American guitarist David Rea, who by then had joined Ian and Sylvia's band. "I would go down there and he'd be all by himself. We'd sit together, the two of us, and we'd play for a little bit. I had him all to myself. I was just a kid and I felt very lucky to be in the presence of living history. He would make up a riff and I'd play along with it... He knew that I was interested in learning and seeing what he was doing."

When the Home of the Blues closed in late June, a different version of its short history emerged in *The Globe and Mail.* Johnson had simply been under contract to the Left Bank, according to the club's owner, Peter Hill, until he — Johnson — appeared one evening in June at another Yorkville coffeehouse. "That night there was not one paid admission to the Home of the Blues," Hill explained. "I didn't think it was fair of him to put himself in competition with the club so I let him go."

Johnson claimed to *The Globe and Mail* that he was owed $700 in back pay and expenses. Hill was quoted in the same article as saying that the terms of his agreement with Johnson had changed after the first three weeks and that Johnson's reckoning was based on his mistaken assumption that the original contract remained in effect. Hill acknowledged that Johnson had spent $149.48 of his own money to refurbish the room, but added that the investment — a far cry from $7,000 — simply offset a debt that Johnson had owed him. "My books," he concluded, "show we're pretty well even."[4]

They also left Johnson pretty well broke.

14. "Just some man who fell"

Lonnie Johnson eventually rented a room with a kitchenette in a three-storey row house at 181 Avenue Road, a few doors north of Davenport Road, which in turn was a few blocks north of Yorkville. The flat was small but served Johnson's needs; he owned little and lived alone.

He often filled his days by walking — sometimes in the neighbourhood, heading north and then east along MacPherson Avenue to the liquor store at the old Summerhill railway station, but more often south into the heart of downtown Toronto, with a stop along the way now and then at St. Basil's, a Roman Catholic Church on Bay Street.

He had not gone very far north one Tuesday in 1966 — no farther than the small park beside Avenue Road United Church, three short blocks from his rooming house — when he had a fall.

"I saw him go down, quite a big man," remembered Roberta Richards, who was on her way at the time from her home on MacPherson Avenue to the corner store with her young son, Danny.

"I went over to him. 'Are you okay?'

"'No," he said, 'I'm not okay.'

"He pointed to his right knee. There was a big tear in his pants.

"'I don't know how I can help you,' I said, 'unless you want to come over here to the bench and I'll see if I can clean up your knee.' I thought that was what he was concerned about.

"'I don't care about the knee. I'm on my way to get a job.' He was somewhat agitated, but in a very quiet way. 'I'm on my way to get a job, and you gotta sew this up.'

"'Where do you live?'

"'Oh, not far from here.'

"'Can't you go back and get another pair of trousers?'

"'I don't have another pair of good trousers.'

"So we walked back across the street to my house. You'd never do that now; you'd never take a stranger into your house.

"'You're going to have to remove your pants,' I told him, 'because I don't sew well, and I really don't want to sew them *on* you.' I went and got him a big towel; he put that around himself. It took me forever. It was not a great job, but the pants were together and I cleaned them up as best I could.

"'That's great,' he said. 'I'm going out to get my job now. See ya.'

"When he left, I realized that I didn't even know who he was. And he didn't know who *I* was. I was just somebody who had fixed his pants.

"'Okay,' I said to Danny. 'Back to the store.'

"'Mommy, who was that man?'

"'I don't know, just some man who fell.'

"The next day, about 10:30 in the morning, there was a knock at the door. And there he was with this childish grin, eyes twinkling, and two big containers of ice cream.

"'I brought these for you,' he said, 'and I want to thank you very much. I got my job.'

"I invited him in. He ate a lot of the ice cream, and so did Danny.

"He said, 'Do you like music?'

"'I love music.'

"'That's what I do. I sing a little and I play a little guitar. That's the job I got.'"

15. "Grabbing for jobs"

Lonnie Johnson had gone to see Doug Cole, the owner of four popular nightspots that employed musicians in Toronto: George's Spaghetti House in the former George's Hotel at the northwest corner of Dundas and Sherbourne streets, Castle George upstairs at the same address, and two rooms new in 1966, George's Kibitzeria on Huron Street north of Harbord Street at the western edge of the University of Toronto campus, and George's Italian Villa on Bloor Street West, out near Royal York Road in suburban Etobicoke.

Cole was aware of Johnson's troubles earlier in the summer at the Home of the Blues. "It looked like he was really jobbed," he remembered, echoing the recollections of other people who knew Johnson at the time, notwithstanding the two sides of the story as it was reported by *The Globe and Mail.* "He had no money at all."[1]

Johnson had left the city briefly in late July 1966, travelling to Port Arthur (Thunder Bay) on the northern shore of Lake Superior for a two-week engagement at the Marine Room of the Shoreline Motor Hotel, where he spelled local favourites Merv and Merla, whose act included musical comedy, folk songs and strolling violin and viola duets.[2] Back in Toronto — by one account in the company of a woman he had met in Port Arthur[3] — he saw his prospects remain poor until the end of October, when he joined the lineup of American folksingers and guitarists who regularly appeared at Castle George, among them in this same period Casey Anderson and Tom Pasle.

Once again, Toronto reviewers took note. Arthur Zeldin from the *Star* and, of course, Patrick Scott — nearing the end of his association with the *The Globe and Mail* — climbed the stairs to the medievally appointed second-floor room, with its arched entrance, its leaded glass windows and its heavy wooden doors.

Zeldin summed up his visit in two short paragraphs notable for the questionable observations that Johnson's delivery of the blues was "singularly unbluesy in its effects" and that his ballads, "with their ukulele-like arrangements" recalled Dick Powell's performances in Hollywood musicals from the 1930s.[4]

Patrick Scott found a readier point of reference in Josh White, the popular African-American singer and guitarist who was appearing that same week at Johnson's old haunt in Yorkville, the Penny Farthing. "During the year and a half that Lonnie Johnson has been kicking around Toronto," Scott began, "almost everyone I know who has heard him has come up to me at one time or another and said either 1) 'He's almost as good as Josh White,' or 2) 'He's even better than Josh White.'" Scott went on to point out just how inappropriate such comparisons were, at the same time dismissing them in a way that emphasized Johnson's superiority on virtually every count.[5]

"IT HAS BEEN A TOUGH YEAR," Johnson lamented to David Cobb of the Toronto *Telegram* a few days before Christmas 1966, at which point he was back for a week at Castle George. "I've been grabbing for jobs. I'm still grabbing and I'm not used to that. I don't know what I'm doing from one day to another — I don't know what I'm doing between now and March."

In fact he did not know what he would be doing on Christmas Day. He had gone back to see his family in Philadelphia over the holidays in 1965, but his current job at Castle George ended on Christmas Eve, making a timely departure for home impossible. And so he weighed his options: his apartment was too small to hold a party, he told Cobb, and although he had friends in Scarborough, they were a $5.80 cab ride away — as if that were more prohibitively expensive than a ticket for the bus that he apparently wished so dearly to take to Philadelphia. The implication, in any event, was that he would be on his own; his remarks — like those about his age when he opened the Home of the Blues — sounded rather like a play for sympathy.

Cobb's article, suitably titled "The lonely Christmas of Lonnie Johnson," appeared on December 24 in the *Telegram*'s entertainment supplement *Showcase*,[6] which ran a front-page photograph of an unsmiling Johnson wearing a curly white wig under a Santa Claus hat. The image of a black St. Nicholas apparently took the newspaper's senior editors by surprise when they saw it,[7] and perhaps Johnson as well: the photograph was a composite — a fake.

Johnson returned to Castle George in late January 1967 for a week, and again in March for four. Work was scarce enough in the interim that Johnson's playing on the latter occasion prompted Patrick Scott to offer a rare critical observation, albeit one that he quickly qualified. "The old minstrel's fingers seemed a little out of shape after a lengthy layoff," Scott wrote, "but all of his rhythmic cylinders were functioning fully, and his voice — whether on ballad or blues — remains the most moving single means of expression in music today."[8]

Scott had moved to the *Toronto Star* by then, his place at *The Globe and Mail* taken briefly by John Norris, whose review of the same engagement took a harder line, particularly with respect to Johnson's choice of material. Under the headline,

"Lonnie Johnson returns: lament for a blues artist," Norris began with a brief résumé of Johnson's distinguished history in jazz and blues. "However," he continued, "much of Johnson's work today gives little indication of this heritage. His stock in trade is a collection of sentimental ballads which he performs with skill and sincerity. So it was inevitable I suppose that he should be serenading the diners with *September Song* when I arrived the other night and that the last song of the two sets I heard was his other perennial tear jerker, *I Left My Heart in San Francisco*."

Norris' interest "as a jazz listener," however, lay precisely in Johnson's blues, which he called "the true measure of the man," commenting further that Johnson himself "must sense it because when he's playing the blues there is a heightened concentration, a greater effort in his playing."

Norris found much to like in Johnson's versions of *Mr. Blues Walks* and *Travelling Light*, the jazz standard *Exactly Like You*, the Ellington ballad *Solitude* and an instrumental version of *Danny Boy*. He described the rest of the performance as "quality pop music" and noted that Johnson was "very good at it." But it was not jazz and, as such in Norris' mind, "such a waste of a man's talent."[9]

Be that as it may, it brought Johnson work at Castle George and, in time, the Kibitzeria and the Italian Villa — once the terms of his employment were clarified. According to Roberta Richards, Johnson held a conveniently quaint view of the charges for food and drink that he ran up rather freely in the course of his engagements; Richards had agreed to Johnson's request that she try to find work for him, but not before Doug Cole had alerted her to the issue.

"Doug said, 'Just for further reference, if you book Lonnie into any of my clubs, *no* bar tab.'

"I asked why; I thought maybe he was drinking it.

"Doug said, 'No, he might have one drink a night, if that, but he's sending drinks out, and dinners, to people who are his friends, and on anniversaries and birthdays. So at the end of a week, he owes the club.'"

Apparently Johnson failed to appreciate that the salutation "Compliments of Lonnie Johnson" meant that *he* was responsible for the bill.

"Doug wanted to warn me," Richards continued, "that if I booked Lonnie I should cut out the tab. He said, 'Maybe you can get through to him, because we certainly have tried.'

"On the way home that night, I said to Lonnie, 'That was nice of you to send those drinks out.'

"He said, 'It's on the house. Everything is on the house.'

"'Not exactly on the house.'

"He said, 'How do you figure that?'

"Well, Doug Cole is kind enough to give you your pay, but there's a lot of money that they're losing.'

"Lonnie said, 'But people come back, they love me and they get a free drink, or dinner.'"

For Johnson, in other words, it was simply good business — for him and for the club.

"If," Richards mused, "he *did* 'get' it, and he wasn't a stupid man, he wasn't letting on."

YEARS LATER, DOUG COLE DID NOT RECALL the need to suspend Johnson's bar tab but allowed that it "could have happened." He did, however, remember some of the stories that Johnson told him, one in particular about playing at private parties thrown by Al Capone for his fellow gangsters in Chicago during Prohibition. "And when they were finished," Johnson boasted to Cole, "they'd tuck a $100 bill in my pocket."

Of course Johnson was not often in Chicago during Capone's ascendancy in the late 1920s, and then only briefly, just a few trips at the behest of the OKeh label, including two for public appearances in February and June 1926 and one for a series of recording sessions in December 1927. By the time Johnson had taken up extended residence in the city a few years later, Capone was in jail. Still, it was a good story, as was one of Johnson's other claims to Cole — that he'd had eight wives and 23 children...

Johnson worked on and off at Castle George, the Kibitzeria and the Italian Villa for the rest of his career. He spent extended periods in 1967 and 1968 at the Kibitzeria, which generally presented black performers. Johnson appeared in the early evening on weeknights and occasionally took a turn as the featured artist on weekends.

He found a good friend in the Kibitzeria's manager, Howard Matthews, whose African-Caribbean origins — Matthews was originally from the island of St. Kitts — made him a rarity among Johnson's otherwise predominantly white associates and acquaintances in Toronto. Matthews had been one of the principals of the First Floor Club, a modern jazz room that had flourished on Asquith Street, north and east of Bloor and Yonge, earlier in the 1960s. His wife, Salome Bey, would sing on occasion at the Kibitzeria, as would Al Cromwell; for a time in 1968, Matthews tried an occasional "name" blues policy, presenting such noted Americans as Sunnyland Slim, Willie Dixon, Jesse Fuller, Bukka White and Roosevelt Sykes, though with mixed success.

Even in this company, however, Johnson remained as true to his ballads as to his blues, both of which impressed Helen McNamara, who visited the Kibitzeria toward the end of 1967 in her role as the Toronto correspondent for *Down Beat*.

"His voice, like his guitar playing," she wrote in the Chicago magazine, "possesses a bitter-sweet quality that is most telling on the blues (most of them his own), but it is also impressive when he switches to popular songs, delivered with surprising freshness. Only the songs stay in the past."

One of those songs was in fact quite recent, Johnson's ode to Brenda, his young daughter back in Philadelphia. "More than any other," McNamara concluded, "this lament sums up the Lonnie Johnson of today. It's not often that he gets a chance to see his family. A blues singer has to go where the work is."[10]

16. "He had a knack"

There was more to it than that, of course — more than simply going where the work was. After all, Lonnie Johnson had been in Toronto for at least two years by the time Helen McNamara reviewed his performance at George's Kibitzeria for *Down Beat*.

No, there was also the warmth of the welcome that he had received on his arrival from the city's critics, musicians and fans. But even after his celebrity in Yorkville had waned — even after the failure of the Home of the Blues and the personal setback that it represented — he stayed on. By then, Charlie Gall would suggest, Johnson had simply come to like Toronto and to feel comfortable as one of its residents.

"I think Lonnie may have got a false impression from people like Jim McHarg and myself, being such enthusiasts, as to the extent of the scene up here. But the thing was, he got treated with respect and I think perhaps that had a lot to do with it."

Despite his problems in finding work, Johnson told David Cobb that he would "still rather live here, where people are laughing and talking and happy." The inference was clear: people were not laughing, talking and happy back home in the United States, where race relations had worsened in the mid-1960s as supporters of the civil rights movement clashed, often violently, with white segregationists.

"Things have changed so much down there," Johnson continued. "In the States you ask someone the direction and he looks at you as if to say, 'What the hell you asking me for?' I don't understand this. At least you can be kind to a dog. When they killed [President] Kennedy, that was the last hope for peace among the races, unless his brother [Robert] gets [voted] in..."

At the same time, though, Johnson made it clear that his perspective from Toronto on events stateside was largely apolitical. His reference to "peace among the races" prompted Cobb to broach the subject of Black Power. Was Johnson familiar with the activist Stokely Carmichael, lately in the news as the face of a new militancy in the civil rights movement?

"No," Johnson admitted rather sweetly, "I never heard of Stokely Carmichael. Does he sing? Hoagy I heard of, but Stokely no."[1]

AND THEN, mused Roberta Richards, there were the women. "He stayed here because he found a woman. Well, a series of women. He had a knack. Young women came around to the clubs — *young* women — and they loved him. You *had* to love him. I never met anyone in my life who didn't love Lonnie Johnson."

Always the charmer, Johnson took pride in maintaining a youthful appearance, one enhanced by the twinkle, real and proverbial, in his eye. He dyed the grey out of his hair, dressed with a sharp, if anachronistic sense of style, and resented any description in print that dwelled on his age — *whatever* it was. When approached in the early 1960s for an interview by Charles Keil, he famously challenged the young American musicologist with a question of his own. "Are you another one of those guys," he asked, "who want to put crutches under my ass?"[2]

Toronto writers were generally careful in that regard, although Helen McNamara, in her first review of Johnson at the Penny Farthing for the *Telegram*, referred to him as "an unbelievable 74 years old,"[3] which was likely as close on the high side to the truth as his preferred estimate at the time, 65, was on the low. Remembered Richards, "He told Helen McNamara, 'I won't read your paper anymore if you write about "old" Lonnie Johnson.'"

Of course age, and its corresponding virtue of authenticity, had generally worked to the advantage of the veteran *country* blues singers who had lately seen their careers renewed by the folk-music revival, some a year or two older than Johnson, most a few years younger. But Johnson, who resisted any suggestion that he belonged in such company, saw age as a drawback. "Who," he asked a friend, "is going to hire an old man of eighty?"[4]

Not, of course, that *he* was 80. And not, in truth, that he really had much in common with his contemporaries. *They* were raised in small towns and on plantations in the rural south, even if Reverend Blind Gary Davis and Son House eventually moved north, and Jesse Fuller to the west coast. Johnson was from New Orleans — a city boy from the first.

"Compared to most of the blues singers who visited Toronto," observed John Norris, "he was much more sophisticated. Their world and my world, with most of them, were so far removed from each other that there was really nothing, or very little, that either had in common. How do you talk to someone like Bukka White, who had been in prison for shooting someone and had no education whatsoever? He's an extreme example, but I remember we went to Guelph [in January 1967], and he was really nervous because there were white women around. He was almost afraid; even though he was in Canada, you could tell he was really unsure."

Not so Johnson, not at all. He was hesitant only to the extent that he took care not to get *too* involved with the women in his life, stopping short of living with any one of them in Toronto. "That would never happen," Richards averred. "There were too many. He would have gotten caught. It was hard to keep track of them."

Most, she admitted, were "really nice," but some were simply after his money. Johnson suggested as much to Marci McDonald of the Toronto *Star*, casting himself in the role of the blues singer who had lived the life that he described in his songs — a role that McDonald helpfully fleshed out with quotes in a suitably evocative, if syntactically tortured vernacular. "When you got money and a woman," she quoted him as saying, "they's got both hands and both feets in your pockets, and when they step out of them, boy, they ain't much left."

But Johnson also revealed to McDonald that he had once returned to Philadelphia unannounced and found his wife with his best friend, as if a cliché of the blues had come to life right before his eyes. And so he stayed on in Toronto, where interviewers knew a good tale of woe when they heard it.

Asked by McDonald where the blues came from, Johnson replied, "From here," touching his heart. "From livin' and from laughin' and from troubles," he continued. "From havin' a wife and losin' her, from havin' money and losin' it all. You'd be surprised when that door closes behind a musician what he has [left]. Heartaches[,] that's what."

To which McDonald added the crowning touch. "A big sad tear," she wrote, "rolls down his cheek."[5]

17. "I'm a Canadian artist now"

Lonnie Johnson often walked from his flat at Avenue Road and Davenport down to Sam the Record Man on Yonge Street. There, past the bins of singles and LPs by the Beatles, Rolling Stones, Mamas & Papas, Monkees and other rock and pop acts of the day, he would climb the worn wooden stairs to the second floor where, under John Norris' vigilant eye, the store kept its extensive stock of jazz, blues and folk LPs.

Norris was careful to guard the integrity of his department's collection against the taint of commercialism. "It was a grey area whether something should be there or be sent back downstairs," he explained, "whether it was more folk music, for example, than pop music. We had Bob Dylan upstairs, and all of those people, but we sent the really commercial stuff — the Kingston Trio, things like that — back downstairs. There would be big debates. We'd say, 'No, we don't want that up here, send it back down.' Of course Lonnie was there in the blues section."

And now Johnson was occasionally there in person to ask how his records were selling, a question that he posed one afternoon to a startled Stuart Broomer, who was working behind the sales counter. "He was wearing a tight-brimmed, round-domed fedora," Broomer later marvelled, "and an old-fashioned suit — box shoulders and wide, short lapels, all of it in a kind of peacock blue — with a vest. Just an extraordinary looking man."[1]

Though still a teenager, Broomer was already writing long essays about Albert Ayler, Ornette Coleman and other avant-garde figures for *Coda Magazine* and had embarked on a performing career of his own, first as a bassist and then as a pianist on Toronto's rather modest free-jazz scene. In later years a noted critic and author, he himself served from 2001 until 2004 as the editor of *Coda Magazine*.

For the moment, though, he was startled by the man standing before him — first by his appearance, then by his identity. "I wasn't aware of Johnson's presence in Toronto, or if I was, it wasn't something I'd thought about. I thought about him primarily as someone who made records in the 1920s with Louis Armstrong and Duke Ellington. Suddenly he's introducing himself to me to query his record sales."

The records in question would have included *Stompin' at the Penny* and likely Johnson's various LPs from 1960, 1961 and 1962 for Bluesville, including *Blues and Ballads* with Elmer Snowden, *Idle Hours* with Victoria Spivey and the solo set *Another Night to Cry* — as well, perhaps, as an album from 1963 for the Danish label Storyville, *Portraits in Blues*. Their sales, Broomer admitted, "probably weren't all that significant," which would have made Johnson all the more adamant that Sam's should promote them properly.

To that end, he occasionally went up to see Sam Sniderman himself in his third-floor office. "He'd have it out with Sam about why his records weren't in the store window," remembered Roberta Richards. "Sam boasted that he really pushed Canadian artists, so Lonnie would go up and challenge him. 'Well, I'm a Canadian artist now,' he'd say. 'I live here. How come my albums are upstairs when they should be down there?' I went with him a few times. We'd walk up those rickety stairs to Sam's office and he'd corner Sam. 'See, my records are still up here. They should be downstairs!'"

18. "History itself walked in"

The International Association of Jazz Record Collectors held its fourth annual convention, July 20 and 21, 1967, at the Alley Cat Club, a discotheque on Richmond Street near Bay Street in Toronto's business district. Lonnie Johnson was a guest the first night, a Thursday; his services at George's Kibitzeria that week were required only on Friday and Saturday.

The convention, co-chaired by the two Canadians among the IAJRC's 18 founding members, brothers Gene and Keith Miller, brought together upwards of 100 collectors from both sides of the border to buy, sell, trade and, of course, play old 78 RPM jazz and blues recordings, and to consider and correct the minutiae of their history. Alexander Ross, writing under the name Cameron Darby in the Toronto *Telegram* the day after the convention, described it rather colourfully as "an orgy of jazz necrophilia," but also made it clear that while he was amused by the jazz collectors' obsession, he was impressed by the erudition that invariably went with it.

Johnson's presence at the convention allowed Ross to point up what he saw as the paradox of the IAJRC's preoccupations. "History itself walked in," Ross wrote of the moment, late on the 20th, when Johnson arrived, carrying his guitar in a vinyl bag. "He has a deep, wise face, and he looks like he's spent all of his life in a succession of strange furnished rooms. Somebody grabbed a microphone and introduced him by saying 'Lonnie was one of the greatest guitar players who ever lived... Uh, and *still is.*'"

Most of the collectors, though apparently not all, turned their attention Johnson's way as he listened intently to the recording of *Broken Levee Blues* that he had made for OKeh in March 1928. "And just for a moment," Ross noted pointedly, "the International Association of Jazz Record Collectors forgot about their discographies, their transcriptions, their disputed personnel lists, their endlessly accumulating collections, and remembered what jaz[z] was all about."[1]

Even so, according to Keith Miller,[2] Johnson had been invited to the convention in part to resolve a dispute over the personnel of Blind Willie Dunn's Gin Bottle Four, the ad hoc group with which he, Dunn — Eddie Lang — and three other musicians recorded for OKeh in 1929. The Gin Bottle Four's significance far exceeded its output — just two sides, *Jet Black Blues* and *Blue Blood Blues* — largely on the basis of the presumed identities of the three other musicians, precisely the sort of details that so concerned the IAJRC's members. But those identities were now uncertain, none more than that of the band's lone horn player. Was it the patriarchal New Orleans cornetist King Oliver, as cited in the IAJRC's bible, *Jazz Records 1897-1942*, compiled by the British discographer Brian Rust? Or was it the popular trombonist Tommy Dorsey, taking a rare turn on trumpet, as Dorsey himself had claimed to one of the IAJRC's principals, the Pittsburgh collector Ken Crawford?

Surely Johnson would know. After all, he appeared on the record. But if the only surviving musician from that session *did* know — if he remembered after nearly 40 years — he was no more forthcoming than he had been in response to the questions that Charlie Gall and Joe van Rossem had asked about his work with Louis Armstrong during the same period, as reluctant as ever to bear witness to his own illustrious past — or perhaps simply to dwell on events that had taken place longer ago than he cared to admit.

Came time to perform, however, he was somewhat more accommodating, "bending backwards a bit," as John Norris put it in *Coda Magazine*, with "a casual half-hour set in which he delighted everyone with some of his better blues and song renditions."[3]

His real concern was far more immediate: how to get home from the Alley Cat Club and, perhaps better still, how not to make the trip alone. He remembered that Keith Miller's wife Doreen, who was handling registration at the front door, had mentioned in passing that she was a fan of his and had heard him a few times at the Penny Farthing. "Well maybe, young lady fan," he said to her when he was ready to leave, "you could drive me home, because I don't have a car or money for a taxicab." She called a taxi instead, gave Johnson $20 from the convention's cash box and sent him safely on his way alone.[4]

19. *Teardrops to My Eyes*

Lonnie Johnson returned to New York once, and perhaps more than once, in 1967. At some point during that year, possibly in December,[1] he went into a recording studio with Moses Asch, whose Folkways label, then in its 20th year, had developed a historically invaluable catalogue of ethnic music from around the world, with a strong representation of American folk, blues and country performers.

Johnson recorded 23 songs and a brief interview for Asch, enough for two LPs eventually issued in 1982 by Folkways, *Tears Don't Fall No More* and *Mr. Trouble* — each with the subtitle *Blues and Ballads* and reissued together 11 years later by Smithsonian Folkways on a single CD, *Lonnie Johnson: The Complete Folkways Recordings*. According to Samuel Charters' notes for the CD, the recordings were in fact intended as a demo for Verve Records,[2] which might explain Asch's decision not to release them sooner on Folkways. And Johnson's choice of material certainly showcased his range very well for any label looking to expand its roster: eight pop standards and 13 blues, most of the latter his own songs, as well as a spiritual of sorts, *That Lonesome Road*, and an instrumental, *Lazy Mood*.

His pop material included *Rockin' Chair* (mistitled *Old Rocking Chair*), *Summertime*, *How Deep Is the Ocean*, *Looking for Another Sweetie*, *What a Difference a Day Makes*, *I Can't Believe that You're in Love with Me* and the inevitable *My Mother's Eyes*. His blues numbered a few of his recent items, notably

Mister [or *Mr.*] *Trouble* — a variant, with extra verses, of the song that he had recorded as *Mr. Blues Walks* with the Metro Stompers — and the revealing *Teardrops in My Eyes*.

But he also revisited some of the songs that he had recorded early in his career — songs as old as *Falling Rain Blues* from his very first session in 1925 and *Careless Love* from 1928. To that end, he enlisted the help of a friend in New York, Bernie Strassberg, who later wrote, "I remember sitting up through half the night listening to some of his old sides from the Thirties [sic] and copying down the words he had now forgotten. This was for a Folkways session redoing some of the old material. I marveled at the way he rhymed — his speech pattern, totally unlike the way most of us would conceive of rhyming. In the studio he did the session in one take."[3]

The varying recording levels from one tune to the next, differing with respect to the degree of presence that they offer Johnson's voice and guitar, suggest that there may in fact have been more than one session. In any event, there were definitely two very different Johnsons in the studio, one a crooner and the other a bluesman.

He sang his favoured ballads in a small, light, thin and at times almost cloying voice, his delivery touched with something of an Irish tenor's sense of theatricality. In turn, he presented his usual blues themes of love lost, love found, betrayal, loneliness and temptation with a darker and more despairing intensity. There was little left in the way of innuendo to his lyrics at this point in his career, as if life by then was far too short to waste on playing word games with sentiments that might be better expressed plainly.

Instrumentally, his blues had become *pro forma*. He repeatedly played the same well-worn patterns over the standard 12-

bar cycle of chord changes, although they were again his *own* patterns, with a half-step modulation up at the ninth bar, an artful turnaround in the 12th and, as often as not, a final, ascending cadence that resolved on the performance's last notes. His breaks and solos varied from one song to the next, but they too were assembled and reassembled from his familiar, and now finite, assortment of licks and lines. For the most part, however, he retained his dexterity, notwithstanding an uncharacteristically sloppy rendition of *Careless Love* in which his guitar work was clumsy and the instrument itself noticeably out of tune. He was at his most inventive when freed from the strictures of the blues altogether — on *Summertime*, for example, and *Lazy Mood.*

In Johnson's mind, of course, these were just his latest recordings; he could not know that they would be his last. Only in retrospect does one song seem to hold particular significance, *Teardrops in My Eyes* — or, more accurately, *Teardrops to My Eyes*, as taken from the second line of the first verse, "Why it bring teardrops to my eyes." While the other blues that he sang for Moses Asch dealt in generalities, this one was both specific and personal, its lyrics speaking directly and with tenderness, as well as regret, to a woman Johnson affectionately called "little kitten" in his second verse and "Susie" in his fifth.

So best wishes to you little kitten
See you some rainy day
I found out you don't love me baby,
Might as well be on my way ...

Goodbye little Susie
It was so nice knowing you.

Maybe you can find yourself somebody,
Can do the things I failed to do.

Coincidentally or not, Susie was the name of the woman he had left in Philadelphia.

20. Room at the Top

They were quite a sight, the two of them — Bill Smith, a tall, slim Englishman with a fondness for tweed suits, and Lonnie Johnson, shorter but in his own way no less a man of fashion — motoring in Smith's white, 1957 convertible Porsche Speedster, top down, through the streets of Toronto's toniest neighbourhoods.

Smith, a freelance photographer by profession, had arrived from London in 1963 and soon joined John Norris at *Coda Magazine*, initially as its art director and latterly as its co-publisher. It was under Smith's influence that *Coda Magazine* extended its editorial embrace to avant-garde jazz during this period, but he himself remained respectful of the music's veterans, among them Johnson, whose celebrity in Toronto — and perhaps his apparent novelty as an elderly African-American bluesman — brought him invitations to parties in Rosedale and Forest Hill. Invitations, evidently, to perform.

"He would do what he normally did," Smith later recalled. "He would sit on a chair and play guitar and sing. I think he was just invited to be there; I'm not sure that he was *hired*... I guess people would give him money. I never really understood that part of it."

Nor was it entirely clear what appeal Johnson, or even the blues *per se*, might have had in such affluently hip — and inevitably white — social circles, save perhaps in some patronizing sense as a charming diversion. "The blues have always been liked *casually* by people," Smith would suggest years later. "They don't have to actually know anything about them to say, 'Oh, I *love* the blues. B.B. King is my favourite.' You know, *that* kind of thing. I think there was a lot of that there."

Certainly Johnson's significance was lost on many, if not most of his listeners at these soirées. "People would gather around," Smith remembered, "but they talked — like they always did." Smith was nevertheless honoured to pick Johnson up in Yorkville, drive him east into Rosedale or north to Forest Hill, and then make sure he got home safely. "To *me*," Smith explained, making it clear that he understood Johnson's significance, even if no one else at these gatherings did, "turning up with someone I considered to be a legend was like turning up with Louis Armstrong."[1]

JOHNSON AGAIN FACED a moneyed, if perhaps less exclusive, crowd when he left George's Kibitzeria in January 1968 for the Room at the Top in the Gaslight Restaurant on Yorkville Avenue at Old York Lane. Unlike the coffeehouses nearby — the Penny Farthing directly across the street, for example, and Johnson's former Home of the Blues a few doors east — the Gaslight was a licensed establishment whose immodestly attired "Gaslight Girls" were among the first in Toronto to be modelled on Hugh Hefner's famous Playboy Club "Bunnies."[2]

When the Gaslight opened in 1961, it presented young opera singers from the Royal Conservatory of Music in its dining room and cocktail pianists upstairs. By 1967, however, the opera singers had long since left and the Room at the Top, as it came to be known, was booking blues and ballad singers of a certain sophistication, including two other African-American performers based in Toronto, Ada Lee and Almeta Speaks. Johnson stayed there for eight weeks, through late March 1968 — evidently as comfortable in this circle as in any other.

Any other: a fortnight later, he was back at George's Kibitzeria, this time sitting in with Willie Dixon and Sunnyland Slim, the latter just then sporting 36 stitches to his left arm after an "incident" at home in the rough and tumble of Chicago.[3]

21. "Back with Fats"

Lonnie Johnson was not alone among Patrick Scott's favoured jazz musicians in Toronto during the mid-1960s. Don Ewell, who played piano in the Harlem "stride" style and was known for his inventive interpretations of Fats Waller compositions, also benefitted from Scott's advocacy. Ewell made his home in Pompano Beach, Florida, but worked regularly in Toronto between the spring of 1965 and the fall of 1968, taking three long engagements at the Golden Nugget and a few shorter bookings at the Colonial Tavern. Scott began to sing Ewell's praises even before he had arrived in the city, describing his playing on the LP *Free 'n Easy!* in 1963 as being "so good so consistently that his every note is a treasure."[1]

After the opening night of Ewell's first visit to the Golden Nugget, Scott admitted, "Never — and I mean that literally — have I looked forward to a musical event with such keen anticipation... and never, against heavier odds, have my fondest hopes been so completely realized."[2] And in classic Scott style, he subsequently pronounced Ewell's year-long contract at the Nugget "the single most rewarding development on the local jazz scene since the collapse of the House of Humbug,"[3] a doubly dismissive reference to the House of Hambourg, which had been a home to Toronto's modernists at a succession of addresses since the late 1940s.

As it happened, Ewell cut short his engagement at the Nugget in December 1965 after just six months, but he was back in Toronto the following June for a CBC-TV taping with one of the legends of stride piano, Willie "The Lion" Smith, and returned with Smith in September for several more weeks at the Nugget, which provided two baby grands for the occasion. Ewell and Smith were in Toronto yet again in February 1967 at Patrick Scott's personal behest to record an LP that Scott financed, produced and ultimately issued as *Grand Piano*, the first and only item on his own Exclusive label.

Ewell also performed at the Nugget with several other guests, including singer Olive Brown and clarinetist Henry Cuesta together, as well as saxophonists Eddie Barefield, Buddy Tate, Earle Warren and Bud Freeman individually in quick succession, and — twice during the summer of 1968 — Lonnie Johnson.

Toronto fans were used to hearing Johnson on his own; his association with the Metro Stompers had lasted only for about six months, and intermittently at that, ending with the recording session for *Stompin' at the Penny*. But Johnson had often worked with pianists earlier in his career, dating back to his years in New Orleans and St. Louis with his brother James and continuing on record and in clubs with such greater and lesser figures as John Arnold, De Loise Searcy, Porter Grainger, Putney Dandridge, Roosevelt Sykes, Lil Armstrong, Blind John Davis, Claude Hopkins and, as recently as 1963 on the LP *Portraits in Blues*, Otis Spann.

Johnson added yet another, and altogether surprising, name to that list, one as illustrious as it was improbable, when, in paying tribute to Don Ewell's skill at the Golden Nugget, he remarked to Alastair Lawrie of *The Globe and Mail*, "I close my eyes and I'm back with Fats." The compliment, wrote Lawrie, was "offered with sincerity and sadness by a man who was with

Fats Waller when he died."[4] It was a good story, like many that Johnson told, but Waller had in fact died of pneumonia on a train near Kansas City, with only his manager present, en route back to New York in December 1943 from a solo engagement in Hollywood.

Still, Johnson and Ewell were an effective match musically, one that apparently put Johnson's Kay electric guitar on greater display instrumentally than usual.[5] They were also a hit with local fans, according to Patrick Scott. "Of all the performers the Nugget has teamed with pianist Don Ewell since inaugurating its guest-star policy," Scott noted pointedly in the Toronto *Star*, "the one who's done the best business is Lonnie Johnson, who was in the wings all the time."[6]

22. "He was unrecognizable"

Lonnie Johnson started the day — March 12, 1969, a Wednesday — as he often did, with a meal at Webster's, a neighbourhood restaurant on the northeast corner of Webster Avenue and Avenue Road. Johnson lived just a short block and a half to the north; Yorkville Avenue was a longer block to the south.

Webster's, which stayed open all night, had achieved a certain notoriety in the Village as — in the words of one of its regular patrons, David Rea — "a place of assignations and god knows what else. We all used to have breakfast at Webster's, at least until the place got too hot and there were more cops in there than anybody else."

Among musicians, of course, "breakfast" could mark either the end of a long night's work or, for Johnson, the start of a new day. A chilly day in this instance — with the temperature just below freezing and the skies overcast, conditions that would have hardly kept Johnson from his usual walk downtown after he had paid his bill at Webster's. He had the afternoon to himself; he was working nightly at George's Italian Villa in Etobicoke and looking ahead to a studio date with Jim McHarg's new Clyde River Jazz Band for Toronto's Arc Records.[1]

Johnson had just left Webster's when a car turning east on to Webster Avenue from Avenue Road struck a car travelling west on Webster itself. The impact of the collision sent one of the vehicles up over the curb and onto the sidewalk, crushing Johnson against the wall of the restaurant.

THE DOCTOR ON CALL at Toronto General Hospital that afternoon dialled the telephone number that Johnson carried as a contact in case of emergencies — Roberta Richards' number. Assuming that Richards was Johnson's daughter, he informed her that her father had been seriously injured in a traffic accident and asked that she come to the hospital as soon as possible.

"It was the old part of Toronto General," Richards remembered, "an old, grey holding area, for want of a better term, with cots on both sides of the room. I walked through there three times. I couldn't find my dad. So I went out to the nurses' station and said, 'My father's not in there.' They said, 'Of course he is.' They took me to this man. He was unrecognizable... They said, 'This is your father.' I looked at him and I looked at him. Then I saw Lonnie's name at the foot of the bed."

News reports in the days following variously suggested that Johnson had suffered a fractured hip or leg, kidney damage and severe bruising. He was expected to be hospitalized for at least four months.[2]

23. "No one said 'No'"

The benefit concert for Lonnie Johnson at the Ryerson Theatre on May 4, 1969, was the third in 16 months to be held in Toronto on behalf of a jazz musician in distress.

The first, organized by Patrick Scott and Jim McHarg in aid of Don Ewell, took place at the Colonial Tavern on December 17, 1967; Ewell had suffered a mild stroke a few days earlier during an engagement at the Yonge Street club with Willie "The Lion" Smith. Johnson was announced as one of the evening's performers — along with Smith, pianist Claude Hopkins, the Metro Stompers, Olive Brown and Henry Cuesta — but was in fact in New York at the time, possibly in a recording studio with Moses Asch.[1]

The second, organized by Howard Matthews, Helen McNamara and others for Archie Alleyne, followed at the Town Tavern on January 21, 1968; Alleyne had been seriously injured in an automobile accident a month before. This time, Johnson did perform, albeit somewhat out of place on his own among bands led by several of the leading lights of the modern Toronto jazz scene, including pianist Brian Browne, with whom Alleyne had been working, as well as vibraphonist Hagood Hardy, valve trombonist Rob McConnell, flugelhorn player Fred Stone and composer Ron Collier.[2]

Ewell and Alleyne both recovered and in due course resumed their careers. But Ewell was 51, and Alleyne had just turned 35. Johnson's future was less certain; he was at least 69, possibly several years older, and alone in a foreign country. Quite apart from being unable to support himself during his convalescence, he would have a substantial hospital bill to pay. Like Ewell and Alleyne, though, he had many friends and supporters, including Lady Iris Mountbatten, who brought together a benefit committee for a meeting at her suite in the Sutton Place Hotel, and Richard Flohil, who agreed to produce the benefit itself.

Lady Iris, a distant member of British royalty, had moved in 1965 from New York to Toronto on the occasion of her marriage to the Canadian actor William Kemp. The couple separated almost immediately, but Lady Iris remained in the city for the rest of her life, counting Johnson and such visiting jazz "royalty" as Count Basie, Duke Ellington and Earl Hines among her friends.[3]

Richard Flohil had arrived in Toronto from England in 1957 and within weeks made his first trip to Chicago and its famed South Side blues clubs. He, too, contributed to *Coda Magazine* in its early years and latterly presented concerts by Sleepy John Estes, Muddy Waters and others at the First Floor Club, and by B.B. King at Massey Hall — all the while working as an editor and publicist.

"For the Estes thing," Flohil explained in a 1970 interview, "we talked 50 people into putting up $10 each. We paid Estes $300 for three days' work, plus his transportation and lodging, and at the end we gave back the 50 investors $9.25 each."[4]

Flohil had known as a teenager in Yorkshire of Lonnie Johnson's jazz recordings with Louis Armstrong and Duke Ellington; he first saw Johnson himself, singing ballads and blues, at London's Festival Hall in 1952. Some 17 years later, Johnson, though still singing ballads and blues, was thriving at least in part through his association with the *folk* revival.

How appropriate, then, that the range of artists that Flohil and the benefit's other organizers invited to perform should have reflected the width and breadth of Johnson's career and influence — from John Lee Hooker, who was in Toronto from Detroit to sing the blues at the Riverboat that week, to Sir Charles Thompson, who was working at the King Edward Hotel — from Ian and Sylvia with their new, country-rock band, the Great Speckled Bird, to Sonny Greenwich, whose stirring, avant-garde solos owed a debt, conceptually, to the linearity that Johnson had introduced to jazz guitar more than 40 years earlier.

Three members of the Saints and Sinners, trombonist Benny Morton, saxophonist Rudy Powell and drummer George Reed, made a quick detour to Toronto en route to an engagement the following night in Cleveland; singers Salome Bey, Olive Brown, Jodie Drake and Almeta Speaks all performed, as did the Metro Stompers and the bands of Henry Cuesta, Hagood Hardy and pianists Ian Bargh and Connie Maynard. Cuesta absolutely insisted on being allowed to participate even though organizers had already extended invitations to more than enough performers.[5]

"No one said no," recalled guitarist Leigh Cline, whose company, Festival Sound, handled the concert's technical aspects. "Everybody wanted to play." Well, *almost* everybody, Richard Flohil admitted years later, revealing that a noted Canadian singer and songwriter had declined but made a generous donation — insisting on anonymity — instead.[6]

The concert ran for more than five hours, drawing an audience upwards of 1,000. John Norris, who was assisting backstage, subsequently reported the tally, after expenses, as $2,855.30,[7] a not inconsiderable sum at the time, and especially important as Johnson's hospitalization proved to be three times longer than initially estimated.

24. “His door was always open”

Valerie Speirs had heard Lonnie Johnson with Don Ewell at the Golden Nugget in the summer of 1968, stopping in at the club for nothing more than a quick bite and ultimately staying much longer under the spell of his performance. By coincidence, she too was now in Toronto General Hospital; by coincidence, her room was across the hall from his.

Informed of his presence, she went over to visit as soon as her own recovery allowed. “His door was always open,” she wrote soon after in *Coda Magazine*.[1] The walls of his room were hung with cards from well-wishers; a guitar leaned at the ready in one corner.

She found Johnson bedridden and in traction, “white plaster as far as the eye could see.” He called her “Darling” and they talked about the jazz greats he had known, Louis Armstrong in particular.

“Louis and I are the oldest jazz musicians left around now,” he lamented; word had it that Armstrong, who was in New York’s Beth Israel Hospital with serious health problems of his own, would no longer be playing trumpet. “But I’m going to get out of here,” Johnson vowed, reviewing his own prospects. “I’m over the worst of it, and I want to get out and kiss the good green earth one more time.”

As it happened, Armstrong did not stop playing — not completely. And Johnson was not over “the worst of it” — not at all. For the moment, though, his condition appeared to be improving.

"One afternoon," Speirs wrote in *Coda Magazine*, "I heard the old Lonnie Johnson from across the hall. Sheer, superb blues singing — complete with guitar strapped across his paining chest. He was singing beautifully. I walked in and found just about everyone in the wing who could walk — even one eager patient holding his intravenous bottle over his head."

Johnson sang for a long time, pausing only for sips of ginger ale as he took one request after another from the crowd that had gathered in his room. "Old things and new," according to Speirs, "happy blues and quiet."

When she later complimented him on his courage and praised his will to live, he looked heavenward, and said, no, it had nothing to do with him, his fate was in God's hands. And when, with her own health restored, she returned a month or so later to Toronto General to visit him again, she learned that he had suffered further complications. His door was now closed.

25. "It was really quite sad"

Lonnie Johnson had three strokes at Toronto General Hospital in the course of 1969. The first was mild, the second and third more severe. For a time, he convalesced under Roberta Richards' care at her home on MacPherson Avenue, with assistance from the Victorian Order of Nurses and from Howard Matthews, who sent over food and, as required, helping hands from the Underground Railroad, a restaurant that he, Archie Alleyne and others had just opened at its first location on Bloor Street East.[1]

Johnson's third stroke paralyzed his left side, extending his recovery well into 1970 and taking him by the turn of the new year to Riverdale Hospital, which specialized both in rehabilitation and in chronic care.

Richards went to see Johnson almost daily. Lady Iris Mountbatten was also a regular vistor, as was Vernon Clapp, an Ontario Hydro clerk who had befriended Johnson soon after his arrival in Toronto and had taken him on fishing trips to lakes in the Kawarthas and up near North Bay. Clapp was not in the best of health himself, but proved to be a stalwart during the months of Johnson's hospitalization.

"He loved Lonnie and wanted to keep him cheered up," marvelled another of Johnson's frequent visitors, the singer and guitarist Mose Scarlett, "so he used to make up these monthly calendars — every day had a different saying, or a little joke, or a cartoon — and he made sure they got to Lonnie so he had something to look forward to."[2]

Scarlett, then in his early twenties, was just beginning to move from folk music to the blues, jazz and Tin Pan Alley classics that, together with his amiable bass-baritone, would bring him a modest following for the next 40 years. Like Johnson, he was one of the artists on Roberta Richards' roster; at her behest, he often cashed the cheques she wrote for Johnson on the bank account that held the proceeds from his benefit. Johnson in turn gave most of his stipends to the women in his life, both real and imagined, in the latter instance falling for the ruse of lonely hearts clubs that took money in return for risqué photos of women who purportedly were also in search of love.

"They would always write that they wished they had a certain type of perfume," Scarlett explained of the ploy, "but it was expensive, like $50, so Lonnie'd put the money in an envelope and send it off to them. They'd send him more pictures. He put the pictures in a little pencil case that he used to keep under his pajama shirt. When I'd go to the hospital, he'd show them to me. I knew he was being 'taken,' but you couldn't tell him that."

But better, in Johnson's case, the fantasy than the reality: his girlfriend in Toronto at the time of his accident was controlling and abusive. "She came around each Saturday," Scarlett remembered, "mostly because she'd get thrown in the Don Jail for being drunk and disorderly on Friday night. They'd let her out in the morning, and then she'd go over to the hospital and demand money from Lonnie. He'd give her the rest of what he had left."

Johnson's visitors were otherwise increasingly few and far between as his convalescence lengthened from weeks to months. Inevitably, he began to feel forgotten, which only made him all the more determined to recover.

"This was a very even-tempered man," Richards observed, "a very quiet man. He was funny, hilarious, a very gentle man.

But he seemed to be getting... I don't want to use the word 'depressed,' because I didn't know much about depression then... but he seemed to getting a little... *despondent*... because people weren't coming to visit him and he didn't understand why. In his mind, he was still the great Lonnie Johnson. So why wouldn't they come? He started telling me things like, 'I'm never going to die in the hospital. You make sure of that. And I *am* going to perform again.'"

Realistically, he might *sing* again — and in fact he did — but the paralysis to his left side, his arm and hand included, made it unlikely that he would also be able to play guitar again, much less play it in the style and with the assurance that had so influenced the history of the instrument in blues and jazz. Still, he tried.

"His guitar was in the closet," Scarlett recalled, "and every once in a while he'd ask the nurse to get it for him. It was really quite sad. I'd put the strap around him. He sort of felt like he could play the guitar, but his hands would just hang over it."

Johnson had the instrument out again one day when Lady Iris and her son Robin were visiting. "He was very badly crippled," she later told CTV's *W5*, "but he tried to play. He started to play for Robin, and he played a blues. And then the tears came to his eyes. 'I'm sorry Robin, I'm sorry. I just can't.'"[3]

His prospects nevertheless began to improve at Riverdale Hospital, where he took physiotherapy to regain some of the motor skills that he had lost. "We knew that he would never fully recover," Richards admitted, "but I hoped, and I'm sure lots of other people hoped, that if he got the left arm back... His speech was not impaired and his right hand was great; if he could get his chording hand back, then he could at least sit and play."

Johnson, of course, shared Richards' hope, and indeed was sustained by it through the worst of his ordeal. "I want to get well," he told Helen McNamara when she stopped in to see him on one of his darkest days. "I want to do one more farewell trip to Europe and then I want to come back here to live."[4]

26. "A space around every note"

Richard Flohil's first major production, a concert by B.B. King at Massey Hall on Valentine's Day, 1969, had been a success. Suitably encouraged, he followed up a year later with Blue Monday, an evening — February 23 — that would offer Toronto fans a survey of the music in its various forms, styles and traditions, both old and new.

Flohil initially planned to have Magic Sam Maghett on the bill, but the young Chicago guitarist and singer, just 32 years old, died of a heart attack in December 1969. Flohil also lined up Son House, only to learn that the veteran Delta bluesman had fallen asleep in a Rochester snowbank after a few too many drinks and suffered frostbite to his fingers.[1] Flohil did have a firm commitment from Otis Spann — his presence was advertised right up to the day of the concert, along with that of the Memphis soul singer Bobby "Blue" Bland, the flashy Chicago guitarist Buddy Guy and a young Toronto band, Whiskey Howl — but the pianist wound up instead at Chicago's Cook County hospital with perforated ulcers. Flohil also asked Lonnie Johnson if he might be able to appear. Yes, Johnson said, he might.

His health had continued to improve as 1969 turned into 1970 to the point where, on weekends, he could take day trips from Riverdale Hospital to visit Roberta Richards, Howard Matthews and Salome Bey, Mose Scarlett and others. It was important that he remain calm while on these furloughs, Richards explained, "but of course once he got out, he was very excited.

He wanted to see people, go places, catch up on what was going on."

He was out on just such a jaunt at the start of January when B.B. King, arriving in Toronto a day in advance of a show at the Rock Pile, called Flohil from the Lord Simcoe Hotel to ask if he — Flohil — knew of Johnson's whereabouts. Johnson had of course been one of King's early and most important influences.

"I said, 'No, B., but I could check,'" Flohil recalled of their conversation. "So I called Howie Matthews.

"I said, 'Howie, do you know where Lonnie Johnson is?'

"He said, 'Yeah, he's in my kitchen.'

"I said, 'You're kidding! May I bring B.B. King over immediately? They've never met!'

"So I drove downtown from Willowdale in my rusty Toyota, picked B. up and went to Howie's place, which at the time was on a little street off Homewood Avenue, near Jarvis. Tiny house. We walked in, said hello to Howard, went into the kitchen and there was Lonnie Johnson."

Lonnie Johnson — and also Sonny Terry and Brownie McGhee, who were in town for an engagement at the Riverboat. "They knew B. and introduced him to Lonnie."

The historic significance of the meeting left Flohil, passionate blues aficionado that he was, quite dazed. "I felt as though I had no business being there. When I tell this story, people say, 'What did they talk about?' Don't ask me!"

Flohil did not put Johnson's name on the ads for Blue Monday that soon began to appear in Toronto newspapers, but Johnson's presence at Massey Hall was an open secret during the days immediately preceding the concert. On February 19, with four days to go, Melinda McCracken took note in *The Globe and*

Mail of the concert's official lineup and added, "Lonnie Johnson, the Toronto bluesman who is still recovering from an accident and a stroke, will be on hand too,"[2] leaving open the exact nature of his participation. An item on the 20th in the same newspaper's "Weekend in Toronto" listings was clearer: "Lonnie Johnson, injured last year in an accident, will be there, though he won't perform."[3]

Whatever the plan, it meant that Johnson, with Roberta Richards' help, had to extend his latest day trip from Riverdale Hospital by an extra 24 hours — well into Monday night. He was "very shaky" by the time he arrived at Massey Hall, Richards remembered, and yet defiant in response to her suggestion that he should use his cane when he went out onstage.

And there was no doubt at all in his mind that he *would* perform once he got there. The only question concerned the other musicians who would be involved; for the first time in a career of more than 55 years he was unable to accompany himself. But Buddy Guy was "more than thrilled," in Richards' words, by the opportunity to back up a musician who had been so central to the history of the blues. And Jim McHarg, also on hand backstage, was no less willing to assist, though he could only borrow an electric bass for the purpose, an instrument to which he was not accustomed.

If Johnson was concerned at all, it was about the time. He preferred not to stay up past 11:30, or so he told Peter Goddard of the Toronto *Telegram*. Whiskey Howl and Buddy Guy had gone on first and second, respectively, followed by an intermission. It was getting late. "But," Goddard noted in a rather cryptic reference to Johnson's indomitability, "he'd gone through so many things, he would like doing something more."

To a worried Richards, whom he suggested join her friends in the audience, Johnson said simply, "You're going to see the best show of your life."

Richard Flohil went out onstage after the break and reviewed the problems he had encountered in booking the evening — first Magic Sam's death, then Son House's misfortune in Rochester and finally, at the 11th hour and now to the surprise and disappointment of the Massey Hall audience, Otis Spann's absence due to poor health.

"Flohil sighed," wrote Peter Goddard. "The crowd sighed, and waited for what was next. Whatever was expected couldn't have been as moving as what happened."

Flohil introduced Johnson, who made his way slowly to centre stage, cane in hand after all, with Buddy Guy, Jim McHarg and Guy's drummer, Fred Below. The audience stood as one in welcome, its cheers growing with his every, unsteady step. Bobby Bland and the members of his band slipped out into the shadows at the rear of the stage to watch, sensing the significance of the occasion.

"Lonnie got out there," Richards remembered, "looked around, saw everybody and got this great big grin, like nothing had ever happened. His legs seemed to stabilize. He got to the stool and smiled at Buddy Guy, calm as could be."

With the audience awed and suddenly silent in his presence, he began to sing, his warm, sweet tenor filling the hall. Guy, so histrionic in his own set, played for Johnson as if Johnson was playing for himself. Time seemed to stand still. Years later, Wayne Wilson of Whiskey Howl recalled, "There was a space around every note that Lonnie sang that seemed to underline the eternity of the moment."[4]

Lonnie Johnson and Buddy Guy, Massey Hall, Toronto, February 23, 1970.
Photograph by Bill Smith. Courtesy Bill Smith.

Johnson offered just two songs, *Careless Love* and *Tomorrow Night*, and then, to an ovation even more tumultuous than the one that had greeted his arrival, started toward the rear of the stage.

"All the kids were on their feet," Goddard reported. "Johnson stopped, transfixed by the sound. They were grabbing for his hands. And still he stared, only to slowly move on again."[5]

Slowly, and with tears streaming down his face.

27. "He'd had enough"

Richard Flohil lost $1,200 on the show — $1,200 that he didn't have — and, as he would tell people for years after, he stopped smoking the next day as a result.

Buddy Guy was indeed more than thrilled to have played for Lonnie Johnson at Massey Hall; he eventually purchased a print of a Bill Smith photograph from the evening — Johnson, supporting himself with his cane as he sang from a stool; Guy watching in awe as he played from a chair to Johnson's left — and hung it proudly at home in Chicago. Proudly, but with more than a touch of humility.

"I think my mouth is just wide open at watching him play [sic], instead of me trying to play," he told Holger Petersen of CBC Radio's *Saturday Night Blues* in 2008. "When he came out I was just so emotionally high, I don't think I played worth a damn that night."[1] To the contrary, Peter Hatch, reviewing the concert for *Coda Magazine*, suggested that Guy had "played beautifully, reminding me at times of Lonnie's accompaniments of Texas Alexander many years ago."[2] Guy always did have a talent for mimicry.

Johnson, meanwhile, was understandably elated by his reception. He had not been forgotten after all. "You can get me more bookings," he announced to Roberta Richards. "I'm going to resume my career."

His first step was to leave Riverdale Hospital. "I think he'd had enough," Richards admitted. "He was better. He could walk with a cane. We had discussions about him leaving. He said, 'I want to get my own place.'"

Johnson checked himself out on April 1, 1970,[3] and moved into a small, sparsely furnished apartment on Sherbourne Street, not far from George's Spaghetti House and Castle George to the south, and just a little farther from the home of Howard Matthews and Salome Bey, off Sherbourne to the north.

28. "He came up and he sang"

Still very much the sport, his hair black, his jacket and slacks casual, Lonnie Johnson caught Jim Galloway's eye from a table to the left of the stage at the Savarin one night in early May. He had his guitar by his side.

Galloway, yet another of the Scottish jazz musicians who dominated the traditional scene in Toronto during the 1960s, was leading the Metro Stompers in their first appearance at the Savarin, a large supper club on Bay Street north of Adelaide Street in Toronto's business district. The clarinetist and soprano saxophonist had joined the Stompers in 1967 and replaced Jim McHarg as their leader in 1968. McHarg in turn soon formed another band that found work at the Constellation Hotel, out on the airport strip northwest of the city.

Dixieland, and indeed jazz of any description, had long since left Yorkville by 1970. So, too, by and large, had the neighbourhood's hippie counterculture, its idealism giving way to the alienation of a more desperate, though still youthful, community watched closely by local officials, particularly the police, and waited out by real-estate developers whose plans called for a reinvention of the Village as a fashionable shopping district; the two Victorian homes that housed the Penny Farthing would be among only a dozen or so original buildings that remained on Yorkville Avenue between Bay Street and Avenue Road when, in the summer of 2009, a small historical plaque was mounted near the site of what had once been the Riverboat and what had since become the southwest corner of the five-star Hazelton Hotel and its adjoining boutique condominium, where suites listed in the millions of dollars.

Toronto nightlife had also started to change during Johnson's year of convalescence. His old haunts were still open, but Castle George and George's Kibitzeria had both turned exclusively to modern jazz, the former the domain in 1970 of pianist Brian Browne and the latter operating under new management as Meat and Potatoes, with two young American musicians recent to Toronto, pianist Ted Moses and the guitarist known

Lonnie Johnson, with Jim Galloway (left) and Charlie Gall, The Savarin, Toronto, May 1970. Courtesy Jim Galloway.

simply as Muñoz, among its regular attractions in the spring and early summer.

Johnson was in effect left to start all over again, dropping in unannounced on musicians of his acquaintance and hoping that they would ask him to perform. His visit to the Savarin, just weeks after he left Riverdale Hospital, may have been his first such foray.

"When I noticed that Lonnie was there," Galloway remembered, "I said, 'Would you care to join us?' I'm not sure how he came to be there. He wasn't on his own. There were people with him, but I don't remember who they were; my attention was on Lonnie. And he came up and he sang."[1]

In fact he sang just one song, possibly his last in public, *My Mother's Eyes*.

29. "A matter of time"

Lonnie Johnson did not sing when he stopped by CBC-TV's *Luncheon Date* on May 7, 1970, a few days one side or the other of his visit to the Savarin. *Luncheon Date* was strictly a talk show; if the musicians among Elwood Glover's guests were to perform — David Rea and the American soul singer Solomon Burke were also booked that week, along with various arts, sports and media personalities[1] — they would have had to be paid.

Johnson's appearance was nevertheless a small step toward a comeback, a way of getting the word out locally about his release from hospital and his readiness to return to work. As if to alert viewers to the importance of the elderly African-American gentleman who appeared on their TV screens with his sad eyes and broad smile, *Luncheon Date* arranged for two executives from Broadcast Music Inc. — Edward M. Cramer, its president, and Harold Moon, the general manager of its Canadian operation — to present Johnson with the organization's Commendation of Excellence.[2]

Johnson took a much more significant step forward in his return to performance with a booking to appear on August 9 at the second annual Ann Arbor Blues Festival in Michigan; he was scheduled between Buddy Guy and Otis Rush in an afternoon concert that was also to feature country bluesman John Jackson, pianist Little Brother Montgomery and harmonica player Carey Bell.[3] Given the festival's success in its first year, and the expectation that it would continue to flourish in its second, the engagement offered Johnson a wonderful opportunity to show the blues world that he was still a vital performer.

It also gave him three months to regain at least some of the facility that he had lost as a guitarist. He was taking therapy for his fingers[4] and, as *Coda Magazine* later reported, thought it only "a matter of time" before he could play again.[5]

He would not live long enough to make his prediction come true.

"THE LAST TIME I SAW HIM, a few days before the end," wrote his friend Vernon Clapp *in memoriam*, "he was kneeling on the floor of his apartment playing with two kittens and laughing so hard he could hardly talk to me."

It was a side of Lonnie Johnson that Clapp had seen many times before. "I found it hard to associate him with the blues," Clapp admitted. "He was always laughing."[6]

This was the private Lonnie Johnson, of course, the Lonnie Johnson known to his friends, not the Lonnie Johnson portrayed by the media — not the man who had obliged David Cobb of the Toronto *Telegram* and Marci McDonald of the Toronto *Star* with the stories of loneliness and tough luck that he thought journalists wanted to hear. "They look for me mostly to tell the hardships of my life," he had suggested in 1967, speaking of his experience with writers in general, "instead of the best part of my life..."[7]

Those hardships remained a central theme in the various accounts of his life and career that appeared in Toronto newspapers after his body was found in his Sherbourne Street apartment on June 16. The *Telegram* reported that he had died "alone, and broke" and suggested that his existence in Toronto had been "hand-to-mouth."[8] The *Star* described him as "virtually broke,"[9] although it also quoted Jim McHarg in a separate article as saying that Johnson in fact had some money both on his person and in the bank, as well as a life-insurance policy for $1,000 with the Toronto Musicians' Association.[10] And Helen McNamara referred to him as "the loneliest of men" in her appreciation for the *Telegram*, but immediately qualified that assertion with another, "and the most optimistic" — thus capturing the paradox of the musician she had come to know during the previous five years.[11]

One story in the *Star*[12] suggested that Johnson had died on the evening of the 15th, but the 16th, a Tuesday, was quickly adopted as his official date of death. His body lay unclaimed in the city morgue on Lombard Street until the 18th while local authorities tried, initially without success, to contact his family in Philadelphia. They finally allowed Johnson's friends in Toronto, with the support of the musicians' association, to have him transferred first to the Rosar Morrison Funeral Home for visitation and then, on the morning of the 20th, a Saturday, to Our Lady of Lourdes Roman Catholic Church for mass. Roberta Richards, acting as Johnson's designated next of kin, handled the details; Jim McHarg, who assumed for himself a central role in the proceedings, dealt on his own with the press and was credited in some reports with all of the arrangements that were made on Johnson's behalf.[13]

Johnson's family, duly located, arrived in time for the funeral; Susie, her brother and little Brenda were among the 80 or so friends, fans and fellow musicians who gathered at Our Lady of Lourdes, along with representatives from the *Star*, the *Telegram* and the CTV public affairs show *W5*. After a 45-minute service, which concluded with Salome Bey singing *Tomorrow Night* and *My Mother's Eyes*, accompanied by guitarist

Ed Bickert, Johnson's coffin was carried from the church by pallbearers Howard Matthews, Archie Alleyne, Jim Galloway, Stan Thomas, Billy O'Connor and Mickey Shannon,[14] Thomas a Toronto folksinger, O'Connor a local booking agent for whom Johnson had worked, and Shannon the acting president of the musicians' association.

The cortège proceeded to Mount Hope Catholic Cemetery, where those in attendance were surprised to learn that there would be no interment; Johnson's relatives insisted that his body be returned to Philadelphia instead, a development that prompted Patrick Scott, now writing in his capacity as the *Star*'s television critic about the *W5* tribute that aired the following day, to refer darkly and without elaboration to "the whole sickening circus of death — complete with its ghastly behind-the-coffin contest for possession of the corpse."[15]

It was, in its suddenness and apparent insensitivity, an unfitting end to the Toronto chapter of Johnson's life. That he would be repatriated — that there would be one last trip way down that lonesome road[16] — was nevertheless a proper conclusion to the story of one of the true originals in American music.

30. "After all the days"

Buddy Guy returned to Massey Hall on his own in 2005, and annually each spring for several years thereafter. By then he was one of the music's most popular figures, a showman whose performances were a blend of the proverbial old, borrowed and blue, personalized largely by a flamboyance that was his alone.

He spoke of Lonnie Johnson during some of these concerts. On one occasion, he paid tribute at great length to his old acquaintance. On another, in April 2010, he mentioned Johnson's name only in passing. As the audience stirred in recognition, he added proudly, and to a growing chorus of applause, shouts and whistles, "I played with him on this stage."[1]

Just as Lonnie Johnson had wished: still remembered after all the days he's gone.

Discography 1965-1970

Stompin' at the Penny with Jim McHarg Featuring Lonnie Johnson, Columbia EL 110
Johnson (guitar, vocals), McHarg (bass), Eric Nielson (clarinet), Charlie Gall (cornet), Ron Simpson (banjo), Bernie Nathan (drums).

Toronto, 24 November 1965

China Boy
Mr. Blues Walks (LJ, vocal)
Bring It on Home to Mama (LJ, vocal)
West End Blues
Go Go Swing
My Mother's Eyes (LJ, vocal)

Seven other titles without Johnson. Reissued on CD in 1994 as *Lonnie Johnson Stompin' at the Penny with Jim McHarg's Metro Stompers*, Columbia CK 57829.

Tears Don't Fall No More, Folkways FS 3577
Johnson (guitar, vocals)

New York City, 1967

Raise Your Window High
Tears Don't Fall No More
Long Road to Travel
Prisoner of Love

Careless Love
Juice Headed Baby
Old Rocking Chair
When You Always by Yourself
Lazy Mood (guitar only)
My Mother's Eyes
Summertime
See See [or *C.C.*] *Rider*

Reissued on CD in 1993 as part of *Lonnie Johnson: The Complete Folkways Recordings*, Smithsonian Folkways SF 40067.

Mr. Trouble, Folkways FS 3578

same session

Mr. Trouble
You Have My Life in Your Hands
How Deep Is the Ocean
Pouring Down Rain
The Entire Family Was Musicians
Falling Rain Blues
Teardrops in [sic] My Eyes
Looking for a [sic] Sweetie
I've Been a Fool Myself
What a Difference a Day Makes
That Lonesome Road
I Can't Believe

Reissued on CD in 1993 as part of *Lonnie Johnson: The Complete Folkways Recordings*, Smithsonian Folkways SF 40067.

End Notes

Preface

1 "A belated wake for Lonnie" [hand-printed invitation from Vernon and Muriel Clapp], collection of Roberta Barrett. The wake was held 1 November 1970 at the Clapp residence in Etobicoke.

2 Mark Miller, *Cool Blues: Charlie Parker in Canada, 1953* (Toronto: Nightwood Editions, 1989).

3 Lonnie Johnson, quoted in Samuel Charters, "Lonnie Johnson's Blues" [liner notes], *Lonnie Johnson: The Complete Folkways Recordings* [CD], Smithsonian Folkways SF 44067 (1993), unpaginated [3].

"An authentic living legend"

1 Advertisement, Toronto *Telegram*, 20 May 1965, 35.

2 Advertisement, Hamilton *Spectator*, 11 April 1963, 23.

3 Sheila Gormley, "Yorkville's Friday faces," *After Four* [Toronto *Telegram*], 13 May 1965, 9.

4 Adil. [Sid Adilman], "Richard & Mimi Farina," *Variety*, 2 June 1965, 60.

5 Patrick Scott, "Yorkville no place for Lonnie Johnson," Toronto *Globe and Mail*, 26 May 1965, 13.

6 Noted in Jimmy McDonough, *Shakey: Neil Young's Biography* (Toronto: Random House, 2002), 121.

7 John Norris, "Around the world: Toronto," *Coda Magazine*, June-July 1965, 14.

"Nice plain people"

1 "Pianist prefers Canada no race stigmas here," Toronto *Telegram*, 4 January 1951, 21.

2 Morgan Winters, "Introducing Calvin Jackson," *New Liberty*, March 1951, 79.

3 "What's happened to: Calvin Jackson," Toronto *Star*, 28 November 1959, 32.

4 Andrew Scott, "T.O. confidential: Toronto's jazz scene in the '50s," *Coda Magazine*, January 2007, 19, 23-25.

5 Verum [sic] Clapp, "I remember Lonnie,"*Jazz Journal*, January 1972, 39.

6 "Oldtime blues singer finds green pastures in Canada," Chicago *Defender*, 1 August 1966, 10.

"Tough to follow"

1 Lonnie Johnson, *Roaming Rambler Blues*, recorded 12 August 1927 for OKeh in New York.

2 Lonnie Johnson, "The entire family was musicians," *Lonnie Johnson: The Complete Folkways Recordings*, track 23.

3 Paul Oliver, *Conversation with the Blues* (Cambridge: Cambridge University Press, 1997), 107, 122, 140.

4 David Cobb, "The lonely Christmas of Lonnie Johnson," Toronto *Telegram*, 24 December 1966, 3; Samuel Charters, *Walking a Blues Road: A Selection of Blues Writing 1956-2004* (London: Marion Boyers, 2004), 123-124.

5 Marci McDonald, "Lonely Lonnie Johnson sings and lives the blues," Toronto *Star*, 5 April 1969, 61.

6 Pops Foster with Tom Stoddard, *The Autobiography of a New Orleans Jazzman* (Berkeley, California: University of California Press, 1971), 92.

7 "An interview with Punch Miller," Laurie Wright, ed., *Storyville 1998-9* (Chigwell, Essex, England: L. Wright, 1999), 156. [Drawn from notes from an interview conducted 1 September 1959 in New Orleans by Richard Allen and "Mac" Fairhurst.]

8 Foster and Stoddard, *Autobiography of a New Orleans Jazzman*, 92.

9 Chris Albertson, "Lonnie Johnson: Chased by the blues," *Bluesland, Portraits of Twelve Major American Blues Masters*, ed. Pete Welding, Toby Byron (New York: Dutton, 1991), 42.

10 M.H.S., "Vaudeville reviews: Palace," New York *Clipper*, 25 January 1922, 9.

11 Ibee., "Palace," *Variety*, 27 January 1922, 8.

12 "Season's best show at Orpheum this week," Winnipeg *Tribune*, 19 September 1922, 11.

13 Oliver, *Conversation with the Blues*, 140.

14 "Here and there among the folks," *Billboard*, 20 October 1923, 57.

15 Johnson's wife, who recorded as Mary Johnson for Brunswick and Paramount in 1929 and for Champion and Decca during the 1930s, was born Mary Smith. If Mary Smith and Mary Hicks were one and the same, then her marriage to Johnson was likely not her first. See "Mary Johnson" in Sheldon Harris, *Blues Who's Who: A Biographical Dictionary of Blues Singers* (New Rochelle, New York: Arlington House, 1979), 287-288.

16 H.T.L. "Vendome Theater," Chicago *Defender*, 8 November 1924, 8; a variation of this review appeared with the byline Hi Tom Long in *Billboard*, 15 November 1924, 49.

17 "Miss Bessie Smith at the Booker Washington Theatre," St. Louis *Argus*, 22 February 1924, 4.

18 Oliver, *Conversation with the Blues*, 122.

19 "Blues singing contest to start at Booker Washington Theatre next Thursday," St. Louis *Argus*, 26 October 1923, 4.

20 "Miss Irene Scruggs wins final blues singing contest," St. Louis *Argus*, 7 March 1924, 4. According to Brian Rust, *Jazz Records 1897-1942* (New Rochelle, New York: Arlington House, 1978), 1376, Scruggs made her first recordings for OKeh on or about 30 April and 1 May 1924. There are no reports in the St. Louis *Argus* of a similar blues contest during the winter of 1924-1925.

21 Washington's Six Aces, with John Arnold, recorded a single title for OKeh in St. Louis on 4 November 1925 (Rust, *Jazz Records*, 1648), which seems, circumstantially, the likely date as well for *Mr. Johnson's Blues* and *Falling Rain Blues*.

22 Advertisement, Chicago *Defender*, 6 February 1926, 6.

23 B.B. King, with David Ritz, *Blues All around Me: The Autobiography of B.B. King* (New York: Avon, 1996), 23.

24 Thomas Brothers, ed., *Louis Armstrong in His Own Words* (New York: Oxford University Press, 1999), 136.

25 Duke Ellington, *Music Is My Mistress* (Garden City, New York: Doubleday and Company, Inc., 1973), 102.

26 Victoria Spivey, "Blues is my business," *Record Research*, July 1970, 9.

27 Henry Townsend, with Bill Greensmith, *A Blues Life* (Urbana, Illinois: University of Illinois Press, 1999), 18-19.

28 Chris Albertson, *Bessie* (New Haven, Connecticut: Yale University Press, 2003), 204. "Loney" Johnson was among the performers advertised in the Chicago *Defender*, 7 December 1929, 10, for the Midnite Steppers' engagement at the Grand Theater, but neither he nor any of the other artists so identified were mentioned in a detailed review of the show that followed in the *Defender*, 14 December 1929, 11, which suggests that Smith had recently changed her supporting cast.

29 Oliver, *Conversation with the Blues,* 145.

30 "Guitars," *Down Beat*, 1 January 1940, 13.

31 Lonnie Johnson, "Working with Lang rated as 'Greatest Thrill' by Johnson," *Down Beat*, May 1939, 16.

32 *Joel Whitburn Presents Top R&B Singles 1942-1999* (Menomonee Falls, Wisconsin: Record Research Inc., 2000), 228.

33 Valerie Wilmer, "Lonnie Johnson talks to Valerie Wilmer," *Jazz Monthly*, December 1963, 5.

34 "Ory leads jazz concert," New York *Times*, 1 May 1948, 19.

35 Gary Fortine, "Lonnie Johnson in Cincinnati (1947-1954)," *78 Quarterly*, Vol. 1, No. 10 (undated), 101-104.

36 Samuel B. Charters, *The Country Blues* (New York: Da Capo, 1975), 85.

37 Albertson, "Lonnie Johnson: Chased by the blues," 40-41.

"Keys to the city"

1 The engagements of The Sparrows [later, The Sparrow], Joni Anderson and the Dirty Shames at the Penny Farthing were listed in the "Coffee houses" column of the weekly "What's going on" page in the Toronto *Telegram* — respectively, 15 May 1965, 18; 8 May 1965, 20; 5 June 1965, 22.

2 John McHugh, interview with the author, 26 June 2009. McHugh denied contemporary accounts that he was in fact present at the New Gate of Cleve, as reported, for example by Patrick Scott in "A metamorphosis in Yorkville," Toronto *Globe and Mail*, 18 September 1965, 16.

3 Jim McHarg, "Lonnie Johnson," *Coda Magazine*, December 1965-January 1966, 2.

4 McDonald, "Lonely Lonnie Johnson sings and lives the blues."

5 All quotes from David Rea have been taken from an interview with the author, 5 November 2009.

6 Patrick Scott, "Johnson deserves keys to city," Toronto *Globe and Mail*, 23 June 1965, 15.

7 Patrick Scott, "Prisoner of the assembly line," Toronto *Globe and Mail*, 23 September 1964, 10.

8 Patrick Scott, "Young guitarist plays with subtlety, taste," Toronto *Globe and Mail*, 8 July 1964, 10.

9 Patrick Scott, "Monk and Hines on the Summit," Toronto *Globe and Mail*, 12 June 1965, 16.

10 Patrick Scott, "The unmentionables receive a mention," Toronto *Globe and Mail*, 3 November 1965, 15.

11 Sid Adilman, "Penny Farthing, Toronto," *Variety*, 7 July 1965, 51.

12 Sid Adilman, "It's a fresh week in slick Village," Toronto *Telegram*, 25 June 1965, 43.

13 Frank Kennedy, "After dark," Toronto *Star*, 3 July 1965, 15.

14 Helen McNamara, "Summer time — and the town is jumping," Toronto *Telegram*, 7 July 1965, 70.

15 McHarg, "Lonnie Johnson."

16 Kennedy, "After dark."

17 McHarg, "Lonnie Johnson."

18 Patrick Scott, "A powerful brew of bottled Stompers," Toronto *Globe and Mail*, 7 July 1965, 13.

19 *Ibid.*

"The stretch of it"

1 Scott, "A powerful brew of bottled Stompers."

2 All quotes from Charlie Gall have been taken from an interview with the author, 1 December 2006. Also, email to the author, 8 May 2007.

"Two old warriors"

1 Patrick Scott, "The offstage Satchmo," Toronto *Globe Magazine*, 7 August 1965, 11.

2 Helen McNamara, "Same old Satchmo but fans love it," Toronto *Telegram*, 20 July 1965, 39; Frank Kennedy, "Satchmo has flashes of brilliance," Toronto *Daily Star*, 20 July 1965, 19; Patrick Scott, "A lean performance from Louis," Toronto *Globe and Mail*, 20 July 1965, 13.

3 Patrick Scott, "An ominous streak shows up in Satchmo," Toronto *Globe and Mail*, 24 July 1965, 13.

4 McHarg, "Lonnie Johnson."

"The picture of sophistication"

1 All quotes from Joe van Rossem have been taken from an interview with the author, 15 December 2009.

2 All quotes from Leigh Cline have been taken from an interview with the author, 14 January 2010.

3 Ron Simpson, interview with the author, 24 June 2009.

4 Marshall Taylor, "TFOADSBRJB," Toronto *Star*, 21 September 1965, 25.

5 All quotes from Ken Whiteley have been taken from an interview with the author, 10 June 2007.

6 All quotes from Chris Whiteley have been taken from an interview with the author, 30 September 2007.

7 Scott, "An ominous streak shows up in Satchmo."

8 McHarg, "Lonnie Johnson."

"Olives akimbo"

1 Patrick Scott, "Even bartenders like Lonnie," Toronto *Globe and Mail*, 18 August 1965, 11.

2 Frank Kennedy, "Great on Yorkville, just so-so on Yonge," Toronto *Star*, 21 August 1965, 24.

3 Frank Kennedy, "Alan McRae's getting ready to click on U.S. market," Toronto *Star*, 4 September 1965, 31.

4 Scott, "Even bartenders like Lonnie."

"Nobody loved music"

1 Cobb, "The lonely Christmas of Lonnie Johnson."

2 Gard., "Belle Claire, Ottawa," *Variety*, 29 September 1965, 50.

"The best Canadian jazz LP of all time"

1 All quotes from John Norris have been taken from an interview with the author, 17 August 2009.

2 All quotes from Bernie Nathan have been taken from an interview with the author, 22 December 2009.

3 Patrick Scott, liner notes, *Stompin' at the Penny with Jim McHarg's Metro Stompers Featuring Lonnie Johnson*, Columbia EL 110 (1966), reissued on CD as *Lonnie Johnson Stompin' at the Penny with Jim McHarg's Metro Stompers*, Columbia/Legacy CK 57829 (1994).

4 John Norris, "Jim McHarg — Lonnie Johnson: A recording for Columbia," *Coda Magazine*, December 1965-January 1966, 31-32.

5 Patrick Scott, "Good listening despite rhythmic rigor mortis," Toronto *Globe and Mail*, 1 December 1965, 12.

6 Patrick Scott, "Johnson goes stompin'," Toronto *Globe and Mail*, 5 February 1966, 16.

7 *Ibid.*

8 Wayne Jones, "Jim McHarg's Metro Stompers," *Coda Magazine*, April-May 1966, 37.

"Brownie was after him"

1 All quotes from Jackie Washington have been taken from an interview with the author, 29 June 2007.

2 All quotes from Roberta Richards (Barrett) have been taken from an interview with the author, 6 July 2007.

3 John Dafoe, "Unique blues happening was the greatest," Toronto *Globe and Mail*, 20 December 1965, 15; Dafoe identified *Falling Rain Blues* as "Rain Keeps Falling Down."

The Blues

1 Barry Callaghan, email to the author, 23 October 2009.

2 John Norris, "Living with the blues — A CBC Taping — Jan. 27-29," *Coda Magazine*, February-March 1966, 27-30.

3 Wilmer, "Lonnie Johnson talks to Valerie Wilmer," 6.

4 Advertisement, Toronto *Star*, 28 January 1966, 20.

"Sing all night, if I want to"

1 Angus Dalrymple, "Jazz singer loves that Toronto atmosphere," Toronto *Star*, 5 May 1966, 42.

2 Patrick Scott, "The blues has many faces — some are in Toronto," Toronto *Globe and Mail*, 14 May 1966, 16.

3 "The best things to do and see," Toronto *Star*, 7 May 1966, 31.

4 "Singer broke contract, owner says," Toronto *Globe and Mail*, 7 July 1966, 10.

"Just some man who fell"

—

"Grabbing at jobs"

1 All quotes from Doug Cole have been taken from an interview with the author, 30 October 2009.

2 Advertisement, Port Arthur *News Chronicle*, 22 July 1966, 6.

3 Jim Christy, "Lonnie Johnson," *Pacific Rim Review of Books*, Fall/Winter 2009, 11.

4 Arthur Zeldin, "Singer has more soul than polish," Toronto *Star*, 1 November 1966, 21.

5 Patrick Scott, "You can't compare Josh and Lonnie, but if you could...," Toronto *Globe and Mail*, 5 November 1966, 17.

6 Cobb, "The lonely Christmas of Lonnie Johnson."

7 Barry Callaghan, email.

8 Patrick Scott, "A little Rich goes a long way," Toronto *Star*, 14 March 1967, 17.

9 John Norris, "Lonnie Johnson returns: lament for a blues artist," Toronto *Globe and Mail*, 15 March 1967, 12.

10 Helen McNamara, "Lonnie Johnson," *Down Beat*, 28 December 1967, 47.

"He had a knack"

1 Cobb, "The lonely Christmas of Lonnie Johnson."

2 Charles Keil, *Urban Blues* (Chicago: University of Chicago Press, 1966), 35.

3 Helen McNamara, "Summer time — and the town is jumping."

4 Clapp, "I remember Lonnie," 39.

5 McDonald, "Lonely Lonnie Johnson sings and lives the blues."

"I'm a Canadian now"

1 All quotes from Stuart Broomer have been taken from an interview with the author, 27 July 2009.

"History itself walked in"

1 Cameron Darby, "The moldy figs," Toronto *Telegram*, 22 July 1967, 12-13.

2 Keith Miller, email to the author, 8 March 2010.

3 John Norris, "Heard and scene: International Association of Jazz Record Collectors — Club Alley Cat, Toronto — July 20 and 21," *Coda Magazine*, September 1967, 32.

4 Doreen Miller, email to the author, 22 March 2010.

Teardrops to My Eyes

1 Johnson's presence in New York at this time was noted by Patrick Scott in "Brilliant jazz benefit concert: A wall-to-wall sellout," Toronto *Star*, 18 December 1967, 25. It is also possible, however, that Johnson could have made an earlier trip in 1967; he appears to have been at least out of work in Toronto, if not out of town altogether, during the late summer, and was reported by John Norris in "Around the world: Toronto," *Coda Magazine*, October-November 1967, 20, to be "all set to depart for Bermuda."

2 Charters, "Lonnie Johnson's Blues," *Lonnie Johnson: The Complete Folkways Recordings*, [7]. At the time, Verve's subsidiary, Verve Forecast, was developing a roster of folk and blues artists that would come to include Tim Hardin, Richie Havens, Lightnin' Hopkins, Leadbelly and Odetta.

3 Bernie Strassberg, notes to *Lonnie Johnson: The Unsung Blues Legend* (CD), Blues Magnet BLM-1001 (2000).

"Room at the top"

1 All quotes from Bill Smith have been taken from an interview with the author, 29 July 2009.

2 "The boom in Bunny Girls," Toronto *Star*, 28 May 1966, 27.

3 Peter Harris, "Two blues shouters of the very highest order," Toronto *Star*, 9 April 1968, 25.

"Back with Fats"

1 Patrick Scott, "Hail! The underprivileged Duke Ellington," Toronto *Globe and Mail*, 23 February 1963, 13.

2 Patrick Scott, "Ewell's piano style memorable," Toronto *Globe and Mail*, 12 May 1965, 9.

3 Patrick Scott, "Babe replaces Olive Brown," Toronto *Globe and Mail*, 15 September 1965, 13.

4 Alastair Lawrie, "Lonnie Johnson closes his eyes, and he's back with Fats," Toronto *Globe and Mail*, 18 June 1968, 12.

5 Helen McNamara, "Rich lode of blues at the Golden Nugget," Toronto *Telegram*, 18 June 1968, 42.

6 Patrick Scott, "Awash in nostalgia at Little Queen Vic's," Toronto *Star*, 27 July 1968, 24.

"He was unrecognizable"

1 Jack Batten, "Sound loud huzzas: the Town reverts to full-time jazz," Toronto *Star*, 18 March 1969, 24; Helen McNamara, "Stompin' up a storm in the Scarboro wilds," Toronto *Telegram*, 20 March 1969, 75.

2 "Jazzman Johnson injured in crash," Toronto *Star*, 14 March 1969, 26; "Lonnie Johnson hit by car," Toronto *Telegram*, 14 March 1969, 78; McDonald, "Lonely Lonnie Johnson sings and lives the blues."

"No one said 'No'"

1 "Jazz stars staging Ewell benefit," Toronto *Globe and Mail*, 15 December 1967, 17; John Kraglund, "Packed benefit concert nets $1,500," Toronto *Globe and Mail*, 18 December 1967, 17; John Norris, "Gimme a pigfoot: a tribute to Don Ewell," *Coda Magazine*, January-February 1968, 16-18.

2 Alan Offstein, "Archie Alleyne benefit," *Coda Magazine*, March-April 1968, 41-43.

3 Peter Goodspeed, "Lady Iris Mountbatten recalled as a 'giving, cherished person,'" Toronto *Star*, 16 September 1982, A13.

4 Jack Batten, "A blues lover's blues," Toronto *Star*, 21 February 1970, 73.

5 Alastair Lawrie, "Another kind of luck for Lonnie," Toronto *Globe and Mail*, 1 May 1969, 10; Melinda McCracken, "Lonnie down, not out with benefit," Toronto *Globe and Mail*, 5 May 1969, 14; Helen McNamara, "Singers and jazz musicians help cure Lonnie's blues," Toronto *Telegram*, 5 May 1969, 25; Don Rubin, "One of the best jazz shows ever," Toronto *Star*, 5 May 1969, 28.

6 Richard Flohil, interview with the author, 12 January 2010.

7 John Norris, "Around the world," *Coda Magazine*, May-June 1969, 33.

"His door was always open"

1 Valerie Speirs, "Another night to cry," *Coda Magazine*, May-June 1969, 31.

"It was really quite sad"

1 The Underground Railroad soon relocated to King Street East, where it flourished for many years.

2 All quotes from Mose Scarlett taken from an interview with the author, 11 April 2010.

3 Lady Iris Mountbatten, quoted on CTV's *W5*, 21 June 1970.

4 Helen McNamara, "Tragedy in his blues," Toronto *Telegram*, 17 June 1970, 82.

"A space around every note"

1 Jack Batten, "A blues lover's blues."

2 Melinda McCracken, "Love and complex thoughts — of these Tim Hardin sings," Toronto *Globe and Mail*, 19 February 1970, 11.

3 "Weekend in Toronto: Pop scene," Toronto *Globe and Mail*, 20 February 1970, 10.

4 Wayne Wilson, email to the author, 29 May 2009. Wilson was Whiskey Howl's drummer.

5 Peter Goddard, "Best blues night since B.B. King hit town," Toronto *Telegram*, 24 February 1970, 72. See also Melinda McCracken, "Blues show turns them on," Toronto *Globe and Mail*, 24 February 1970, 11; Peter Hatch, "This is the blues," *Coda Magazine*, March-April 1970, 31.

"He'd had enough"

1 Buddy Guy, interview with Holger Petersen, November 2008, broadcast on CBC Radio's *Saturday Night Blues*, 1 August 2009.

2 Hatch, "This is the blues."

3 Clapp, "I remember Lonnie," 22.

"He came up and he sang"

1 Jim Galloway, interview with the author, 21 September 2009.

"A matter of time"

1 *Luncheon Date* "union top sheet," CBC archives.

2 John Norris, "Around the world: Toronto," *Coda Magazine*, July-August 1970, 38.

3 Advertisement, *Coda Magazine*, July-August 1970, 35.

4 Clapp, "I remember Lonnie, 22."

5 "Lonnie Johnson," *Coda Magazine*, July-August 1970, 31. This article does not have a byline but was likely written by John Norris.

6 Clapp, "I remember Lonnie, 22."

7 Charters, "Lonnie Johnson's Blues," *Lonnie Johnson: The Complete Folkways Recordings* [3].

8 Peter Goddard, "Farewell to a blues great," Toronto *Telegram*, 22 June 1970, 25.

9 Richard Campbell, "A legend of jazz world Lonnie Johnson dead," Toronto *Star*, 17 June 1970, 50.

10 "Musicians arrange burial of guitarist," Toronto *Star*, 18 June 1970, 28.

11 McNamara, "Tragedy in his blues."

12 "Musicians arrange burial of guitarist."

13 *Ibid.*

14 Richard Campbell, "Guitarist taken to Philadelphia," Toronto *Star*, 22 June 1920, 24.

15 Patrick Scott, "Summer season off to a shaky start," Toronto *Star*, 22 June 1970, 25.

16 Johnson was eventually laid to rest at White Chapel Memorial Park in Feasterville, northeast of Philadelphia.

"After all the years"

1 Buddy Guy, remarks from the stage, Massey Hall, 9 April 2010.

Selected Bibliography

Books

Albertson, Chris. "Lonnie Johnson: chased by the blues." In *Bluesland, Portraits of Twelve Major American Blues Masters*, ed. Pete Welding, Toby Byron. New York: Dutton, 1991.

Charters, Samuel. *Walking a Blues Road: A Selection of Blues Writing 1956-2004*. London: Marion Boyers, 2004.

Crouse, Richard and John Goddard. *Rock and Roll Toronto: from Alanis to Zeppelin* (Toronto: Doubleday, 1997).

Dixon, Robert M.W., and John Godrich and Howard Rye. *Blues and Gospel Records 1890-1943*. Oxford: Clarendon Press, 1997.

Harris, Sheldon. *Blues Who's Who: A Biographical Dictionary of Blues Singers*. (New Rochelle, New York: Arlington House, 1979).

Leadbitter, Mike and Neil Slavin. *Blues Records 1943 to 1970: A Selected Discography*. London: Record Information Services, 1987.

Oliver, Paul. *Conversation with the Blues*. (Cambridge: Cambridge University Press, 1997).

Rust, Brian. *Jazz Records, 1897-1942*. (New Rochelle, New York: Arlington House, 1978).

Articles

Campbell, Richard. "A legend of jazz world Lonnie Johnson dead." Toronto *Star*, 17 June 1970, 50.

— "Guitarist taken to Philadelphia." Toronto *Star*, 22 June 1920, 24.

Christy, Jim. "Lonnie Johnson." *Pacific Rim Review of Books*, Fall/Winter 2009, 11.

Clapp, Verum [sic]. "I remember Lonnie." *Jazz Journal*, January 1972, 39.

Cobb, David. "The lonely Christmas of Lonnie Johnson." Toronto *Telegram*, 24 December 1966, 3.

Dalrymple, Angus. "Jazz singer loves that Toronto atmosphere." Toronto *Star*, 5 May 1966, 42.

Fortine, Gary. "Lonnie Johnson in Cincinnati (1947-1954)." *78 Quarterly*, Vol. 1, No. 10 (undated), 101-104.

McNamara, Helen. "Tragedy in his blues." Toronto *Telegram*, 17 June 1970, 82.

McDonald, Marci. "Lonely Lonnie Johnson sings and lives the blues." Toronto *Star*, 5 April 1969, 61.

McHarg, Jim. "Lonnie Johnson." *Coda Magazine*, December 1965-January 1966, 2.

Norris, John. "Jim McHarg — Lonnie Johnson: A recording for Columbia." *Coda Magazine*, December 1965-January 1966, 31-32.

— "Lonnie Johnson." *Coda Magazine*, July-August 1970, 31. [This article does not have a byline, but is likely by John Norris.]

Wilmer, Valerie. "Lonnie Johnson talks to Valerie Wilmer." *Jazz Monthly*, December 1963, 5-7.

Reviews

Adil., "Penny Farthing, Toronto." *Variety*, 7 July 1965, 51.

Adilman, Sid. "It's a fresh week in slick Village." Toronto *Telegram*, 25 June 1965, 43.

Dafoe, John. "Unique blues happening was the greatest." *The Globe and Mail*, 20 December 1965.

Gard., "Belle Claire, Ottawa." *Variety*, 29 September 1965, 50.

Hatch, Peter. "This is the blues." *Coda Magazine*, March-April 1970, 31.

Kennedy, Frank. "Great on Yorkville, just so-so on Yonge." Toronto *Star*, 21 August 1965, 24.

Lawrie, Alastair. "Lonnie Johnson closes his eyes, and he's back with Fats." Toronto *Globe and Mail*, 18 June 1968, 12.

McNamara, Helen. "Summer time — and the town is jumping." Toronto *Telegram*, 7 July 1965, 70.

— "Lonnie Johnson." *Down Beat*, 28 December 1967, 47.

— "Rich lode of blues at the Golden Nugget." Toronto *Telegram*, 18 June 1968, 42.

Norris, John. "Lonnie Johnson returns: lament for a blues artist." Toronto *Globe and Mail*, 15 March 1967, 12.

Scott, Patrick. "Yorkville no place for Lonnie Johnson." Toronto *Globe and Mail*, 26 May 1965, 13.

— "Johnson deserves keys to city." Toronto *Globe and Mail*, 23 June 1965, 15.

— "A powerful brew of bottled Stompers." Toronto *Globe and Mail*, 7 July 1965, 13.

— "Even bartenders like Lonnie." Toronto *Globe and Mail*, 18 August 1965, 11.

— "Johnson goes stompin'." Toronto *Globe and Mail*, 5 February 1966, 16.

— "You can't compare Josh and Lonnie, but if you could...." Toronto *Globe and Mail*, 5 November 1966, 17.

Liner Notes

Charters, Samuel. "Lonnie Johnson's blues." *Lonnie Johnson: The Complete Folkways Recordings* [CD]. Smithsonian Folkways SF 44067 (1993).

Scott, Patrick. *Stompin' at the Penny with Jim McHarg's Metro Stompers Featuring Lonnie Johnson.* Columbia EL 110 (1966).

Strassberg, Bernie. *Lonnie Johnson: The Unsung Blues Legend* (CD). Blues Magnet BLM-1001 (2000).

Acknowledgements

My efforts to capture something of Lonnie Johnson in his last years — to retrieve him from the realm of legend in blues and jazz history and present him again as a real person — have been assisted by many people in many ways.

By Roberta (Richards) Barrett, Anne Brodzky, Stuart Broomer, Leigh Cline, Doug Cole, Richard Flohil, Charlie Gall, Jim Galloway, Jack King, John McHugh, Marilyn McHugh, Bernie Nathan, John Norris, David Rea, Mose Scarlett, Ron Simpson, Bill Smith, Joe van Rossem, Jackie Washington, Chris Whiteley and Ken Whiteley — who shared with me their personal recollections of Johnson. I thank them for their candour.

By Chris Albertson, Dean Alger, Archie Alleyne, Eddy B(rake), Colin Bray, Barry Callaghan, Jim Christy, Daisy Debolt, Jim Eigo, Amos Garrett, Nicholas Jennings, Maureen Kennedy, David Lee, Doreen Miller, Keith Miller, Roger Misiewicz, Bill Munson, Holger Peterson, Michael Pickett, Ted Roberts, Ron Sweetman, Brian Towers, Rob van der Bliek, David Wilcox and Wayne Wilson — who offered their assistance in various matters of research. I thank them for their courtesy.

By Celia Donnelly and Paula Wilson at *The Globe and Mail*, as well as Roberta Barrett, Charlie Gall, Jim Galloway and Bill Smith, who provided the photographs that appear in *Way Down That Lonesome Road*. I thank them for their generosity.

By Roberta Barrett, Colin Bray, Stuart Broomer, Beverley Daurio, Fern Lindzon, Jack Litchfield, Danny Marks, Ted

O'Reilly, Holger Peterson, Rob van der Bliek and John Wilby, who offered timely encouragement at various points as the project proceeded. I thank them for their support.

By Jack Litchfield and John Wilby, who gave the manuscript a close and informed reading upon its completion. I thank them for their keen editorial instincts, as I do — and have done for my previous six books — Beverley Daurio, my editor at The Mercury Press and Teksteditions. Her continued faith in my writing — in what I choose to write about and how I choose to write about it — has been in equal measure gratifying, reassuring and inspiring.

No funding was sought or received for the research or writing of *Way Down That Lonesome Road.*

INDEX

Notes

Unless otherwise indicated, nightclubs, coffeehouses and other such establishments and institutions are in Toronto

Unless otherwise indicated, italicized entries are titles of songs or instrumental compositions

Photographs have been indexed in italic and bold

CPSIA information can be obtained
at www.ICGtesting.com
Printed in the USA
FSHW022133100121
77566FS

9 780986 869648